Wok & Stir-Fry

Wok & Stir-Fry

Cooking Your Way to Good Living

This edition published by Parragon Books Ltd in 2016
LOVE FOOD is an imprint of Parragon Books Ltd

Parragon Books Ltd
Chartist House
15–17 Trim Street
Bath BA1 1HA, UK
www.parragon.com/lovefood

ISBN 978-1-4748-4995-1

Printed in China

Internal design by Ignition
Additional photography by Charlie Paul (pages 49, 69, 82, 86, 89, 110, 127, 131, 136, 139, 143, 160, 195, 216 & 220)
Additional food styling by Emily Shardlow

Notes for the Reader

- This book uses both metric and imperial measurements. Follow the same units of measurement throughout; do not mix metric and imperial. All spoon measurements are level: teaspoons are assumed to be 5 ml, and tablespoons are assumed to be 15 ml. Unless otherwise stated, milk is assumed to be full fat, eggs and individual fruits and vegetables are medium, pepper is freshly ground black pepper and salt is table salt. A pinch of salt is calculated as $\frac{1}{16}$ of a teaspoon. Unless otherwise stated, all root vegetables should be peeled prior to using.

- The times given are an approximate guide only. Preparation times differ according to the techniques used by different people and the cooking times may also vary from those given.

- For best results, use a food thermometer when cooking meat. Check the latest government guidelines for current advice.

The workhorse of the Chinese kitchen, the wok has been in use for over 2,000 years. Thanks to its unique shape, the wok can cope with virtually all types of food and cooking techniques.

Woks were traditionally made of cast iron, which maintains a steady, even heat. It is worth noting that Chinese cast-iron woks are thinner and lighter than the Western equivalent. They heat up more quickly and also form a more stable layer of seasoning that prevents food from sticking. The downside is that they are prone to shattering if mishandled or dropped. Western cast-iron woks are sturdier but slow to heat up and cool down. Currently, the most commonly used material for woks is carbon steel. Steel woks are relatively lightweight, conduct heat evenly and are quick to heat up. However, they vary widely in price and quality.

Seasoning a Wok
A new steel or iron wok should be scrubbed to remove any rust or factory oil. Place it over a medium heat to dry. While still hot, smear all over with a wad of kitchen paper soaked in cooking oil. Repeat two or three times using clean paper. Allow to cool, then rinse and dry thoroughly.

Cleaning and Maintenance
Wash with hot water but no detergent as this will remove the seasoned coating. Dry over medium heat. Coat with a thin film of oil to prevent rusting.

BASIC TECHNIQUES
Although most often used for stir-frying, the wok can also be used for steaming, boiling, braising, deep-frying, shallow-frying and smoking if fitted with a lid and a stand.

Stir-frying
Before you begin, have all the ingredients measured and prepared. Cut fresh ingredients into small equal-sized pieces so that they cook in the same amount of time. Slicing meat and vegetables diagonally increases the surface area in contact with the hot oil. The wok must be very hot before you add any oil. Use long-handled chopsticks to stir constantly and toss the ingredients so that they all come in contact with the hot oil.

Deep-frying
Use enough oil to give a depth of about 5 cm/ 2 inches. Heat over a medium–high heat until a faint haze appears. If the oil is not hot enough, the food will become soggy instead of crisp. Cook in small batches – overcrowding lowers the temperature of the oil and causes uneven cooking. Remove the food with a wire ladle or tongs and drain thoroughly on kitchen paper.

Braising
Braising is generally used for tougher cuts of meat and dense-fleshed vegetables. The ingredients are briefly stir-fried, then simmered in stock until tender.

Steaming
This method is used in China to cook whole fish, dumplings, vegetables and morsels of poultry and meat. Place the food on a heatproof plate or in a perforated container above boiling liquid in the base of a wok. Cover with a lid to trap the steam, which then permeates the food.

DIPPING SAUCES
These traditional dipping sauces are served with many Asian dishes.

Spring Onion Dipping Sauce
4 tbsp finely chopped spring onions
4 tbsp finely chopped fresh ginger
2 tbsp light soy sauce
1 tsp rice vinegar
4 tbsp rapeseed oil

Combine all the ingredients in a bowl and whisk very thoroughly until well blended. For a smooth sauce, purée in a blender.

Soy-ginger Dipping Sauce
3 tbsp soy sauce
2 tsp very finely chopped fresh ginger

Combine the soy sauce and ginger in a small serving bowl. Leave to stand for 15 minutes to allow the flavour to deepen.

Sweet, Sour & Spicy Fish Sauce
175 ml/6 fl oz Thai fish sauce
100 g/3½ oz granulated sugar
175 ml/6 fl oz lime or lemon juice
1 large garlic clove, crushed, sliced or finely
    chopped
1–2 fresh red bird's eye chillies, sliced

Combine the fish sauce and sugar in a small serving bowl and whisk until the sugar is completely dissolved. Stir in the lime juice, garlic and chillies. Leave to stand for 20 minutes to allow the flavour to deepen.

STOCKS

These essential Asian stocks will give your dishes an authentic flavour.

Basic Chinese Stock

Makes about 1.5 litres/2¾ pints

900 g/2 lb chicken pieces, such as wings, thighs
   and drumsticks, roughly chopped
900 g/2 lb pork spare ribs
450 g/1 lb ham or unsmoked gammon without rind,
   in one piece
4 litres/7 pints water
7-cm/2¾-inch piece fresh ginger, unpeeled and
   thickly sliced
1 celery stick, roughly chopped
1 carrot, roughly chopped
3 large spring onions, green parts included, halved
   lengthways
2 tsp Chinese rice wine or dry sherry

Put the chicken, pork and ham in a large saucepan with enough water to cover. Bring to the boil, then drain in a colander and rinse away the foam under cold running water. Wash out the pan.

Return the meat to the pan with the 4 litres/7 pints of water. Add the ginger, celery, carrot and spring onions, and bring back to the boil, skimming off any foam that forms. Reduce the heat to a very gentle simmer and cook, uncovered, for 2 hours.

Strain the stock through a colander, reserving the liquid and discarding the solids. Pour the liquid through a muslin-lined sieve. Pour back into the pan and add the rice wine. Bring back to the boil, then simmer for 2–3 minutes.

Pour into containers and leave to cool, then store in the refrigerator. Once thoroughly chilled, remove the solidified fat from the surface.

Spicy Beef Stock

Makes about 1.5 litres/2¾ pints

1.5 kg/3 lb 5 oz beef brisket or boneless shin of beef,
   cut into large chunks
3 litres/5¼ pints water
1 small onion, quartered
5-cm/2-inch piece fresh ginger, unpeeled and
   thickly sliced
5-cm/2-inch piece cinnamon stick
5 star anise pods
1 tsp black peppercorns
1 tsp salt

Put the beef in a large saucepan with enough water to cover. Bring to the boil, then drain in a colander and rinse away the foam under cold running water. Wash out the pan.

Return the meat to the pan with the 3 litres/5¼ pints of water. Add the onion, ginger, cinnamon stick, star anise, peppercorns and salt, and bring back to the boil, skimming off any foam that forms. Reduce the heat to a very gentle simmer and cook, uncovered, for 2 hours.

Strain the stock through a colander, reserving the liquid and discarding the solids. Pour the liquid through a muslin-lined sieve. Pour into containers and leave to cool, then store in the refrigerator. Once thoroughly chilled, remove the solidified fat from the surface.

Appetizers

SERVES 4

3 strips of lime zest
2 garlic cloves, peeled
2 slices fresh ginger
1 litre/1¾ pints chicken
    stock
1 tbsp groundnut or
    vegetable oil
175 g/6 oz firm tofu,
    drained and cubed

200 g/7 oz dried fine egg
    noodles
100 g/3½ oz shiitake
    mushrooms, sliced
1 fresh red chilli,
    deseeded and sliced
4 spring onions, sliced

1 tsp light soy sauce
juice of 1 lime
1 tsp Chinese rice wine
1 tsp sesame oil
chopped fresh coriander,
    to garnish

Hot & Sour Soup with Tofu

Put the lime zest, garlic and ginger into a wok with the stock and bring to the boil. Reduce the heat and simmer for 5 minutes. Remove the lime zest, garlic and ginger with a slotted spoon and discard.

Meanwhile, heat the groundnut oil in a large frying pan over a high heat, add the tofu and cook, turning frequently, until golden. Remove the tofu from the pan and drain on kitchen paper.

Add the noodles, mushrooms and chilli to the stock and simmer for 3 minutes.

Add the tofu, spring onions, soy sauce, lime juice, rice wine and sesame oil and briefly heat through.

Divide the soup among four individual serving bowls, scatter over the coriander and serve immediately.

SERVES 4 1 litre/1¾ pints water
2 tsp dashi granules

175 g/6 oz silken tofu,
drained and cut into
small cubes
4 shiitake mushrooms,
finely sliced

4 tbsp miso paste
2 spring onions, chopped

Miso Soup

Put the water in a wok with the dashi granules and bring to the boil. Add the tofu and mushrooms, reduce the heat and let simmer for 3 minutes.

Stir in the miso paste and let the soup simmer gently, stirring, until the paste has dissolved.

Add the spring onions and serve immediately. If you leave the soup, the miso will settle, so give the soup a thorough stir before serving.

SERVES 6-8

2 litres/3½ pints chicken
  stock
2 tsp salt
½ tsp white pepper
2 tbsp finely chopped
  spring onion
1 tbsp chopped fresh
  coriander leaves

wontons
175 g/6 oz fresh pork
  mince, not too lean
225 g/8 oz raw prawns,
  peeled, deveined and
  chopped
½ tsp finely chopped
  fresh ginger
1 tbsp light soy sauce
1 tbsp Chinese rice wine

2 tbsp finely chopped
  spring onion
pinch of sugar
pinch of white pepper
dash of sesame oil
30 square wonton
  wrappers
1 egg white, lightly
  beaten

Wonton Soup

For the wonton filling, mix together the pork, prawns, ginger, soy sauce, rice wine, spring onion, sugar, pepper and sesame oil and stir well until the texture is thick and pasty. Set aside for at least 20 minutes.

To make the wontons, place a teaspoon of the filling at the centre of a wrapper. Brush the edges with a little egg white. Bring the opposite points towards each other and press the edges together, creating a flower-like shape. Repeat with the remaining wrappers and filling.

Bring the stock to the boil and add the salt and pepper. Boil the wontons in the stock for about 5 minutes, until the wrappers begin to wrinkle around the filling.

To serve, divide the spring onion among individual bowls, spoon in the wontons and soup and scatter over the coriander.

SERVES 4

1 litre/1¾ pints chicken stock
175 g/6 oz fresh or frozen sweetcorn kernels

1 tbsp sake
½ tsp sugar
1 tbsp cornflour, blended with 2 tbsp cold water

1 egg white, lightly beaten
2 spring onions, thinly sliced, plus extra to garnish

Sweetcorn Soup

Put the stock in a wok and bring to the boil. Add the sweetcorn kernels and cook for 5 minutes, or until tender.

Strain the stock over a bowl, reserving the stock, and transfer the sweetcorn to a blender or food processor. Process to a purée.

Return the stock to the wok. Press the sweetcorn purée through a sieve into the wok to remove any remaining solid pieces.

Bring to the boil, then stir in the sake and sugar. Add the cornflour mixture and cook, stirring constantly, until thickened. Drizzle in the beaten egg white, stirring in a circular motion, then add the spring onions.

Ladle the soup into individual bowls, garnish with spring onions and serve immediately.

SERVES 4

4 shallots, chopped
1 large garlic clove, chopped
2 tsp finely chopped fresh ginger
1 tbsp groundnut or vegetable oil
450 g/1 lb sirloin steak, external fat removed, cut into 1-cm/½-inch cubes

1.3 litres/2¼ pints Spicy Beef Stock (see page 9)
1 tsp white peppercorns, crushed
150 g/5½ oz dried wide rice noodles
juice of 1 lime
2 tsp Thai fish sauce
½ tsp salt
½ tsp sugar

to garnish/serve
4 spring onions, shredded
1 fresh red chilli, deseeded and cut into thin strips
3 tbsp torn fresh coriander leaves
3 tbsp torn fresh basil leaves
lime wedges

Vietnamese Beef & Noodle Soup

Purée the shallots, garlic and ginger in a food processor or blender, pulsing several times until smooth.

Heat a wok over a medium–high heat, then add the oil. Stir-fry the paste for 2 minutes, taking care not to let it burn. Add the beef and stir-fry for 1 minute, then pour in 1 litre/1¾ pints of the stock. Bring to a rolling boil, skimming off any foam that forms. Add the crushed peppercorns, then reduce the heat and gently simmer for 30–35 minutes, or until the meat is tender.

Meanwhile, soak the noodles in enough lukewarm water to cover for 15 minutes, or cook according to the packet instructions, until tender.

When the meat is tender, stir in any sticky residue that has formed at the edge of the wok. Add the remaining stock, the lime juice, fish sauce, salt and sugar. Simmer for a few minutes.

Drain the noodles and divide among individual soup bowls. Ladle the meat and broth over the top. Scatter over the spring onions, chilli, coriander and basil, then serve immediately with lime wedges.

SERVES 6

450 g/1 lb skinless, boneless cod fillets, cut into large chunks
100 ml/3½ fl oz tamarind concentrate
225 g/8 oz ripe pineapple, cut into bite-sized chunks
1 large ripe tomato, peeled, deseeded and cut into 8 wedges
2 fresh red bird's eye chillies, deseeded and thinly sliced into rounds
1 tbsp Thai fish sauce
12 fresh Thai basil leaves, torn
6 fresh saw leaves, torn, or 5 g/⅛ oz fresh coriander leaves
salt and pepper

light fish stock
2.8 litres/5 pints water
1.1 kg/2 lb 8 oz fish heads and bones
25 g/1 oz fresh ginger, thinly sliced
4 spring onions, crushed
2–3 tbsp Thai fish sauce

Spicy & Sour Fish & Pineapple Soup

For the stock, put the water and fish heads and bones in a large saucepan and bring to the boil over a high heat. Reduce the heat to low–medium, then add the ginger, spring onions and fish sauce and simmer for 1½ hours, or until reduced by about half, skimming off any foam. Strain the stock, discarding the solids, and remove any fat.

Season the fish to taste with salt and pepper. Cover with clingfilm and chill in the refrigerator for up to 30 minutes.

Pour the stock into a wok and bring to a gentle boil over a medium heat. Reduce the heat to low–medium, then add the tamarind concentrate, pineapple, tomato, chillies and fish sauce and cook for 10 minutes. Add the fish chunks and cook for 5 minutes, or until opaque.

Ladle the soup into individual bowls. Scatter over the torn basil and saw leaves and serve immediately.

SERVES 4

225 g/8 oz dried wide rice noodles
700 ml/1¼ pints canned coconut milk
2 fish stock cubes
3 fresh kaffir lime leaves
2 tbsp Thai red curry paste

bunch of spring onions, roughly chopped
2 fresh red chillies, deseeded and roughly chopped
225 g/8 oz raw squid, cleaned and cut into rings

225 g/8 oz large raw prawns, peeled and deveined
handful of fresh coriander, chopped, plus extra leaves to garnish

Squid + Prawn Laksa

Soak the noodles in a saucepan of boiling water for 4 minutes, covered, or cook according to the packet instructions, until tender. Drain, rinse under cold running water and set aside.

Put the coconut milk, stock cubes, lime leaves, curry paste, spring onions and chillies in a wok and bring gently to the boil, stirring occasionally. Reduce the heat and simmer, stirring occasionally, for 2–3 minutes, until the stock cubes and paste have dissolved.

Add the squid and prawns and simmer for 1–2 minutes, until the squid has plumped up and the prawns have turned pink. Add the cooked noodles and the chopped coriander and stir well. Ladle into individual bowls and serve immediately, garnished with coriander leaves.

MAKES 20

6 dried Chinese mushrooms
55 g/2 oz dried fine cellophane noodles
2 tbsp groundnut or vegetable oil, plus extra for deep-frying
1 tbsp finely chopped fresh ginger

100 g/3½ oz carrot, julienned
100 g/3½ oz cabbage, finely shredded
1 tbsp finely sliced spring onion
1 tbsp light soy sauce
85 g/3 oz soft tofu, drained and cut into small cubes

½ tsp salt
pinch of white pepper
pinch of sugar
20 spring roll wrappers
1 egg white, lightly beaten
dark soy sauce, to serve

Vegetarian Spring Rolls

Soak the mushrooms in a bowl of warm water for 20 minutes. Squeeze out the excess water from the mushrooms and chop finely, discarding any tough stalks. Meanwhile, cook the noodles according to the packet instructions, until tender. Drain, rinse under cold running water and drain again. Chop roughly and set aside.

Heat a wok over a high heat, then add the oil. Toss in the ginger and cook until fragrant. Add the mushrooms and stir-fry for about 2 minutes. Add the carrot, cabbage and spring onion and cook for 1 minute. Add the noodles and light soy sauce and stir-fry for 1 minute. Add the tofu and cook for a further minute. Season with the salt, pepper and sugar and mix well. Continue cooking for 1–2 minutes, or until the carrot is soft. Remove from the heat and allow to cool.

Place a tablespoon of the mixture towards the bottom of a spring roll wrapper. Roll once to secure the filling, then fold in the sides to create a width of 10 cm/4 inches and continue to roll up. Seal with a little of the egg white. Repeat with the remaining wrappers and filling.

Heat enough oil for deep-frying in a wok to 180–190°C/350–375°F, or until a cube of bread browns in 30 seconds. Without overcrowding the pan, cook the rolls in batches for about 5 minutes, or until golden brown and crispy. Serve with dark soy sauce for dipping.

MAKES 20

small knob of butter
1 egg, beaten
115 g/4 oz firm tofu, drained
3 tbsp groundnut or vegetable oil
1 tsp finely chopped garlic
55 g/2 oz lean pork, shredded

115 g/4 oz raw prawns, peeled and deveined
½ small carrot, cut into short, thin sticks
55 g/2 oz canned bamboo shoots, drained and shredded
115 g/4 oz cabbage, finely shredded

55 g/2 oz mangetout, julienned
1 tsp salt
1 tsp light soy sauce
1 tsp Chinese rice wine
pinch of white pepper
20 soft spring roll wrappers
2 tbsp chilli bean sauce, plus extra to serve

Soft-wrapped Pork & Prawn Rolls

Heat the butter in a small heavy-based frying pan and add the beaten egg. Swirl the egg until it covers the base of the pan. Cook until the egg has set and is cooked through, then turn out onto a plate. Cut the omelette into strips.

Slice the tofu horizontally into thin slices. Heat 1 tablespoon of the oil in a large frying pan and cook the tofu for 4–5 minutes, turning occasionally, until golden brown all over. Cut into thin strips and set aside.

Heat a wok over a high heat, add the remaining oil and stir-fry the garlic until fragrant. Add the pork and cook for about 1 minute, then add the prawns and stir-fry for a further minute. One by one, stirring well after each addition, add the carrot, bamboo shoots, cabbage, mangetout, tofu and, finally, the omelette strips. Season with the salt, soy sauce, rice wine and pepper. Stir-fry for a further minute, then turn into a large bowl.

Smear a spring roll wrapper with a little of the chilli bean sauce and place a heaped teaspoon of the filling towards the bottom of the wrapper. Roll up the bottom edge to secure the filling, turn in the sides and continue to roll up gently. Cut diagonally into two halves. Repeat with the remaining wrappers and filling. Serve accompanied by a bowl of chilli bean sauce.

SERVES 4

900 g/2 lb mixed vegetables, such as carrots, baby corn, cauliflower, broccoli, mangetout, mushrooms and onions

115 g/4 oz dried fine cellophane noodles
6 eggs
4 spring onions, diagonally sliced
2½ tbsp groundnut or vegetable oil

100 g/3½ oz canned bamboo shoots, drained
200 ml/7 fl oz ready-made sweet and sour sauce
salt and pepper

Sweet & Sour Vegetables on Noodle Pancakes

Prepare the vegetables as necessary and chop into equal-sized chunks.

Soak the noodles according to the packet instructions, until tender. Drain well and use scissors to cut them into 7.5-cm/3-inch lengths.

Beat the eggs, then stir in the noodles, spring onions, and salt and pepper to taste. Heat a 20-cm/8-inch frying pan over a high heat. Add 1 tablespoon of the oil and swirl it around. Pour in a quarter of the egg mixture and tilt the frying pan so it covers the bottom. Lower the heat to medium and cook for 1 minute, or until the thin pancake is set. Flip it over and add a little extra oil, if necessary. Continue cooking until the pancake begins to colour. Transfer to a plate and keep warm while you make three more pancakes.

When you have made four pancakes, heat a wok over a high heat and add the remaining oil. Add the thickest vegetables, such as carrots, first and stir-fry for 30 seconds. Gradually add the remaining vegetables and the bamboo shoots. Stir in the sauce and stir-fry until all the vegetables are tender and the sauce is hot. To serve, spoon the vegetables and sauce over the pancakes.

SERVES 4

150 g/5½ oz tempura mix
4 shiitake mushrooms
4 fresh asparagus spears
4 sweet potato slices

1 red pepper, deseeded
  and cut into strips
4 onion slices, cut into
  rings
groundnut or vegetable
  oil, for deep-frying

dipping sauce
2 tsp mirin
1 tbsp shoyu (Japanese
  soy sauce)
pinch of dashi granules,
  dissolved in 2 tbsp
  boiling water

Vegetable Tempura

To make the dipping sauce, combine the ingredients in a small dish.

Mix the tempura with water according to the packet instructions. Don't try to make the batter smooth – it should be a little lumpy. Drop the vegetables into the batter.

Fill a wok two-thirds full with oil. Heat the oil to 180–190°C/350–375°F, or until a cube of bread browns in 30 seconds. Lift 2–3 pieces of vegetable out of the batter, carefully drop into the oil and cook for 2–3 minutes, or until the batter is a light golden colour. Remove with a slotted spoon, drain on kitchen paper and keep hot while you cook the remaining vegetables.

Serve immediately with the dipping sauce.

SERVES 4

500 g/1 lb 2 oz sweet potatoes
2 garlic cloves, crushed
1 small fresh green chilli, deseeded and chopped
2 fresh coriander sprigs, chopped
1 tbsp dark soy sauce

plain flour, for dusting
groundnut or vegetable oil, for shallow-frying
sesame seeds, to garnish

soy-tomato sauce
2 tsp vegetable oil
1 garlic clove, finely chopped

1½ tsp finely chopped fresh ginger
3 tomatoes, skinned and chopped
2 tbsp dark soy sauce
1 tbsp lime juice
2 tbsp chopped fresh coriander

Sweet Potato Cakes with Soy-tomato Sauce

To make the soy-tomato sauce, heat the oil in a wok and stir-fry the garlic and ginger over a medium heat for about 1 minute. Add the tomatoes and stir-fry for a further 2 minutes. Remove the wok from the heat and stir in the soy sauce, lime juice and coriander. Transfer the sauce to a small bowl and keep warm.

Peel the sweet potatoes and grate finely. Place the garlic, chilli and coriander in a mortar and crush to a smooth paste with a pestle. Stir in the soy sauce and mix with the sweet potatoes.

Put some flour on a plate. Divide the mixture into 12 equal portions, toss each portion in the flour until coated and pat into a flat, round patty shape.

Heat a shallow layer of oil in a wide frying pan. Fry the sweet potato patties, in batches, over a high heat until golden, turning once. Drain the sweet potato cakes on kitchen paper.

Transfer the sweet potato cakes to a serving dish, sprinkle with sesame seeds and serve immediately with the soy-tomato sauce.

MAKES 24

24 gyoza wonton
wrappers
groundnut or vegetable
oil, for shallow-frying
2 tbsp Japanese rice
vinegar
2 tbsp shoyu (Japanese
soy sauce)

filling
100 g/3½ oz Chinese
leaves, finely shredded
2 spring onions, finely
chopped
175 g/6 oz fresh pork
mince

½-inch/1-cm piece fresh
ginger, finely grated
2 garlic cloves, crushed
1 tbsp shoyu (Japanese
soy sauce)
2 tsp mirin
pinch of white pepper
salt

Pork Gyoza

To make the filling, combine all the ingredients in a bowl. Season to taste with salt.

Lay a gyoza wonton wrapper flat on the palm of your hand and put 1 heaped teaspoon of the filling in the centre. Brush a little water around the edges of the wonton wrapper. Fold up the sides to meet in a ridge along the centre and press the edges together. Brush the curved edges of the wrapper with a little more water and make a series of little folds along the edges. Repeat with the remaining wrappers and filling.

Heat a shallow layer of oil in a wok with a lid and add as many gyoza as will fill the bottom of the wok with just a little space in between. Cook for 2 minutes, or until the undersides are browned.

Add water to a depth of about 3 mm/⅛ inch, cover the wok and simmer over a low heat for 6 minutes, or until the wrappers are translucent and cooked. Remove the lid and increase the heat to bubble away any excess water. Remove the gyoza and keep warm while you cook the remainder.

Put the vinegar in a small dish, stir in the shoyu and add a splash of water. Serve the gyoza with the sauce for dipping.

MAKES 12–15

12–15 square wonton wrappers
groundnut or vegetable oil, for deep-frying
snipped fresh garlic chives, to garnish
Soy-ginger Dipping Sauce, to serve (see page 6)

filling

125 g/4½ oz lean sirloin or rump steak, minced
1 spring onion, green part included, finely chopped
2 button mushrooms, finely chopped
1 small garlic clove, finely chopped
½ tsp finely chopped fresh ginger
½ tsp soy sauce
¼ tsp salt
¼ tsp white pepper
⅛ tsp Chinese five-spice seasoning
½ tsp cornflour
½ egg, beaten

Spicy Beef & Mushroom Wontons

To make the filling, combine the minced steak, spring onion, mushrooms, garlic and ginger in a bowl. Mix the soy sauce, salt, pepper, five-spice seasoning and cornflour to a thin paste. Add the paste to the beef mixture, then stir in the beaten egg. Stir with a fork until very well mixed.

Separate the wonton wrappers and place on a tray, rotating each one so one corner is facing towards you. Cover with a clean damp tea towel to prevent cracking. Working with one wrapper at a time, place a slightly rounded teaspoon of filling in the bottom corner, 1 cm/½ inch away from the point. Fold the point over the filling, then roll up two thirds of the wrapper, leaving a point at the top. Moisten the right- and left-hand corners with a dab of water. Fold one corner over the other and press lightly to seal. Repeat with the remaining wrappers and filling.

Heat enough oil for deep-frying in a wok to 180–190°C/350–375°F, or until a cube of bread browns in 30 seconds. Deep-fry the wontons in batches for 4–5 minutes, until golden brown and crisp. Remove with a slotted spoon and drain on kitchen paper. Transfer to a serving platter, garnish with garlic chives and serve immediately with the dipping sauce.

MAKES 24

24 wonton wrappers
groundnut or vegetable
    oil, for deep-frying
fresh garlic chives and
    lime slices, to garnish

filling
175 g/6 oz white
    crabmeat, drained if
    canned and thawed if
    frozen, flaked
50 g/1¾ oz canned
    water chestnuts,
    drained and chopped

1 small fresh red chilli,
    chopped
1 spring onion, chopped
1 tbsp cornflour
1 tsp Chinese rice wine or
    dry sherry
1 tsp light soy sauce
½ tsp lime juice

Crispy Crab Wontons

To make the filling, combine the crabmeat, water chestnuts, chilli, spring onion, cornflour, rice wine, soy sauce and lime juice in a bowl.

Spread out the wonton wrappers on a work surface and spoon an equal portion of the filling into the centre of each wonton wrapper. Dampen the edges of the wonton wrappers with a little water and fold them in half to form triangles. Fold the two pointed ends in towards the centre, moisten with a little water to secure, then pinch together to seal.

Heat enough oil for deep-frying in a wok to 180–190°C/350–375°F, or until a cube of bread browns in 30 seconds. Deep-fry the wontons in batches for 2–3 minutes, until golden brown and crisp.

Remove the wontons with a slotted spoon, drain on kitchen paper and serve immediately, garnished with garlic chives and lime slices.

MAKES 16

100 g/3½ oz raw prawns, peeled and deveined
2 egg whites
2 tbsp cornflour

½ tsp sugar
pinch of salt
2 tbsp finely chopped fresh coriander

2 slices day-old white bread
groundnut or vegetable oil, for deep-frying

Prawn Toasts

Pound the prawns to a pulp using a pestle and mortar or the base of a cleaver.

Mix the prawns with one of the egg whites and 1 tablespoon of the cornflour. Add the sugar and salt and stir in the coriander. Mix the remaining egg white with the remaining cornflour.

Remove the crusts from the bread and cut each slice into 8 triangles. Brush the top of each piece with the egg white and cornflour mixture, then add 1 teaspoon of the prawn mixture. Smooth the top.

Heat enough oil for deep-frying in a wok to 180–190°C/350–375°F, or until a cube of bread browns in 30 seconds. Without overcrowding the wok, cook the toasts prawn-side up for about 2 minutes. Turn and cook for a further 2 minutes, or until beginning to turn golden brown. Drain on kitchen paper and serve warm.

SERVES 4

8 chicken wings, each wing chopped into 3 pieces
5 tbsp groundnut or vegetable oil
6 tbsp Basic Chinese Stock (see page 9)
2 tbsp chopped fresh coriander

marinade
1½ tbsp Chinese rice wine or dry sherry
1 tbsp soy sauce
1 tbsp rice vinegar
1½ tbsp sugar
¾ tsp salt
⅛ tsp Chinese five-spice seasoning

3 tbsp hoisin sauce
1 tsp finely chopped fresh ginger

Glazed Chicken Wings

To make the marinade, combine the rice wine, soy sauce and vinegar in a small bowl. Add the sugar, salt and five-spice seasoning, and stir until dissolved. Mix in the hoisin sauce and ginger.

Put the chopped chicken wings in a shallow dish and pour in the marinade, turning to coat. Leave to marinate for 1 hour at room temperature, or overnight in the refrigerator.

Heat a wok over a high heat, add the oil and, when it is almost smoking, add the chicken wings and marinade. Stir-fry for 5 minutes, then sprinkle with 4 tablespoons of the stock and stir-fry for a further 4 minutes.

Using tongs, transfer the chicken wings to a serving dish and sprinkle with the coriander. Pour off and discard most of the oil from the wok and return to the heat. Add the remaining stock and stir with a wooden spoon until blended, scraping up the sticky sediment. Pour into a small bowl and serve with the chicken wings as a dipping sauce.

MAKES 36

450 g/1 lb fresh lamb mince
1 garlic clove, finely chopped
1 tsp finely chopped fresh ginger
1½ tbsp soy sauce

1 tsp Chinese rice wine or dry sherry
½ tsp salt
½ tsp sugar
½ tsp white pepper
½ tbsp cornflour
1 egg, beaten

groundnut or vegetable oil, for shallow-frying
shredded Chinese leaves and snipped garlic chives, to garnish
Spring Onion Dipping Sauce, to serve (see page 6)

Fried Lamb Balls with Spring Onion Sauce

Combine the lamb, garlic and ginger in a bowl. Mix the soy sauce, rice wine, salt, sugar, pepper and cornflour to a thin paste. Add the paste to the lamb mixture, then stir in the beaten egg. Stir with a fork until very well mixed. Pinch off small pieces of mixture and roll between your palms to form balls the size of large marbles.

Heat a wok over a high heat, add a shallow layer of oil and, when it is almost smoking, add the balls. Fry the balls in batches for 3 minutes, turning halfway through. Drain on kitchen paper.

Arrange a bed of shredded Chinese leaves on a serving platter. Arrange the lamb balls on top and sprinkle with garlic chives. Serve immediately with the dipping sauce.

SERVES 4

1 iceberg lettuce
1 tbsp groundnut or
  vegetable oil
1 onion, finely chopped
1 fresh red chilli,
  deseeded and
  chopped

350 g/12 oz fresh pork
  mince
200 g/7 oz canned water
  chestnuts, drained and
  chopped
3–4 tbsp soy sauce
1 tsp palm sugar or soft
  light brown sugar

1–2 tbsp Thai green curry
  paste
2 tbsp chopped fresh
  coriander, plus extra
  to serve
lime wedges, to serve

Lettuce Wraps

Separate the lettuce leaves, wash well in cold water and shake dry. Place all the leaves upside down on a large plate and chill in the refrigerator for 2 hours.

Heat the oil in a wok and stir-fry the onion and chilli for 30 seconds. Add the pork and stir-fry for 8–10 minutes, until browned and crisp. Stir in the water chestnuts, soy sauce, sugar, curry paste and coriander and cook for a further 2–3 minutes.

Spoon the pork mixture into the chilled lettuce leaves and transfer to a serving plate. Scatter over the coriander and serve immediately with lime wedges.

SERVES 4

115 g/4 oz broccoli
115 g/4 oz baby carrots, scraped and cut in half lengthways
140 g/5 oz pak choi
1 tbsp groundnut or vegetable oil
1 red onion, sliced
1–2 fresh bird's eye chillies, deseeded and sliced

2.5-cm/1-inch piece fresh ginger, grated
2 whole star anise
1 red pepper, deseeded and cut into strips
1 orange pepper, deseeded and cut into strips

115 g/4 oz baby courgettes, diagonally sliced
115 g/4 oz baby corn, sliced in half lengthways
2 tbsp orange juice
1 tbsp soy sauce
1 tbsp cashew nuts

Warm Asian-style Salad

Cut the broccoli into tiny florets, then bring a small saucepan of water to the boil and add the halved carrots. Cook for 3 minutes, then add the broccoli and cook for a further 2 minutes. Drain and plunge into cold water, then drain again and reserve.

Arrange 25 g/1 oz of pak choi on a large serving platter. Shred the remainder and set aside.

Heat a wok over a medium–high heat, then add the oil. Add the onion, chillies, ginger and star anise and stir-fry for 1 minute. Add the peppers, courgettes and baby corn and stir-fry for a further 2 minutes.

Pour in the orange juice and soy sauce and continue to stir-fry for a further minute before adding the reserved shredded pak choi, broccoli and carrots. Stir-fry for 2 minutes, or until the vegetables are tender but still have a bit of bite. Arrange the warm salad on the prepared serving platter, scatter the cashew nuts over the top and serve immediately.

SERVES 4

8 outer leaves of cos lettuce or similar dark, crisp lettuce leaves
100 g/3½ oz French beans, lightly cooked
100 g/3½ oz baby carrots, lightly cooked
250 g/9 oz salad potatoes, cooked until just tender

1 tbsp groundnut or vegetable oil
125 g/4½ oz fresh beansprouts
8-cm/3¼-inch piece cucumber, deseeded and cut into 4-cm/1½-inch batons
4 eggs, hard-boiled
1 small mild onion, sliced into rings

sauce
4 tbsp canned coconut milk
3 tbsp smooth peanut butter
juice of ½ lime
2 tsp light soy sauce
dash of Tabasco sauce or any chilli sauce

Gado Gado

Roughly tear the lettuce leaves, if large, and arrange on four individual serving plates or a large serving platter. Halve the beans and cut the carrots, as necessary, into batons. Cut the potatoes into chunks if large, then arrange on the plates or platter with the beans and carrots.

Heat a wok over a high heat, then add the oil. Add the beansprouts and stir-fry for 2 minutes, until lightly cooked but still crisp. Remove with a slotted spoon and sprinkle over the cooked vegetables with the cucumber. Peel and quarter the eggs, then arrange on top of the salad.

Add the onion rings to the oil remaining in the wok and stir-fry over a high heat for 5 minutes, or until golden and crisp. Combine all the ingredients for the sauce in a small bowl and pour over the salad. Top with the onion rings and serve immediately.

SERVES 4

4 boneless chicken breasts
2 tbsp Thai red curry paste
2 tbsp groundnut or vegetable oil

1 head of Chinese leaves, shredded
175 g/6 oz pak choi, torn into large pieces
½ head of Savoy cabbage, shredded

2 shallots, finely chopped
2 garlic cloves, crushed
1 tbsp rice vinegar
2 tbsp sweet chilli sauce
2 tbsp Thai soy sauce

Red Chicken Salad

Score the chicken several times and rub the curry paste into each cut. Cover and chill overnight.

Cook the chicken in a wok over a medium heat for 5–6 minutes, turning once or twice, until cooked through. Keep warm.

Wipe out the wok with kitchen paper. Heat 1 tablespoon of the oil in the wok and stir-fry the Chinese leaves, pak choi and cabbage until just wilted. Add the remaining oil, shallots and garlic, and stir-fry until just tender but not browned. Add the vinegar, chilli sauce and soy sauce. Remove from the heat.

Arrange the stir-fried leaves on four individual serving plates. Slice the chicken, arrange on top and drizzle the hot sauce over the dish. Serve immediately.

SERVES 3

2 carrots
2 celery sticks
1 cucumber
200 g/7 oz dried wide
  rice noodles
3 duck breasts, about
  140 g/5 oz each

peanut sauce
2 garlic cloves, crushed
2 tbsp dark brown sugar
2 tbsp peanut butter
2 tbsp coconut cream
2 tbsp soy sauce
2 tbsp rice vinegar

2 tbsp sesame oil
½ tsp black pepper
½ tsp Chinese five-spice
  seasoning
½ tsp ground ginger

Asian Duck & Noodle Salad with Peanut Sauce

Preheat the grill. Cut the carrots, celery and cucumber into thin strips and set aside. Cook the noodles according to the packet instructions, until tender. Drain, rinse under cold water and set aside.

Grill the duck breasts under the preheated grill for about 5 minutes on each side, until cooked through. Leave to cool.

Meanwhile, heat all the ingredients for the sauce in a small saucepan until combined and the sugar has dissolved completely. Stir until smooth.

Slice the duck breasts. Divide the noodles among three individual serving plates. Scatter the reserved carrots, celery and cucumber over the noodles, arrange the duck slices on top and drizzle with the sauce. Serve immediately.

Meat & Poultry

SERVES 4

280 g/10 oz fillet steak, cut into slivers
225 g/8 oz dried medium egg noodles
2 tbsp groundnut or vegetable oil
1 onion, finely sliced
1 green pepper, deseeded and finely sliced

140 g/5 oz fresh beansprouts
1 tsp salt
pinch of sugar
2 tsp Chinese rice wine
2 tbsp light soy sauce
1 tbsp dark soy sauce
1 tbsp finely shredded spring onion

marinade
1 tsp light soy sauce
dash of sesame oil
½ tsp Chinese rice wine
pinch of white pepper

Beef Chow Mein

Combine all the marinade ingredients in a bowl and marinate the beef for at least 20 minutes.

Cook the noodles according to the packet instructions, until tender. Drain, rinse under cold water and set aside.

Heat a wok over a high heat, then add the groundnut oil. Stir-fry the beef for about 1 minute, until the meat has changed colour, then add the onion and cook for 1 minute, followed by the green pepper and beansprouts. Evaporate off any water from the vegetables.

Add the salt, sugar, rice wine and soy sauces. Stir in the noodles and toss for 1 minute. Finally, stir in the spring onion and serve.

SERVES 4

500 g/1 lb 2 oz fillet steak, cut into thin strips
1½ tbsp sesame seeds
125 ml/4 fl oz beef stock
2 tbsp soy sauce
2 tbsp grated fresh ginger
2 garlic cloves, finely chopped

1 tsp cornflour
½ tsp chilli flakes
3 tbsp groundnut or vegetable oil
1 large head of broccoli, cut into florets
1 yellow pepper, deseeded and thinly sliced

1 fresh red chilli, deseeded and finely sliced
1 tbsp chilli oil, to taste
1 tbsp chopped fresh coriander, to garnish

Hot Sesame Beef

Mix the beef strips with 1 tablespoon of the sesame seeds in a small bowl. In a separate bowl, whisk together the stock, soy sauce, ginger, garlic, cornflour and chilli flakes.

Heat a wok with a lid over a medium-high heat, then add 1 tablespoon of the groundnut oil. Stir-fry the beef strips for 2–3 minutes. Remove and set aside.

Discard any remaining oil in the wok, then wipe out with kitchen paper to remove any stray sesame seeds. Heat the remaining groundnut oil, add the broccoli, yellow pepper, red chilli and chilli oil and stir-fry for 2–3 minutes. Stir in the stock mixture, cover and simmer for 2 minutes.

Return the beef to the wok and simmer, stirring occasionally, until the juices thicken. Cook for a further 1–2 minutes.

Transfer to individual serving plates and sprinkle over the remaining sesame seeds and the coriander. Serve immediately.

SERVES 4

1 tbsp groundnut or vegetable oil

1 large dried chilli, deseeded and snipped into 3 pieces

½ tsp Szechuan peppers

100 g/3½ oz fresh beef mince

2 tsp light soy sauce

300 g/10½ oz dried fine rice noodles

chopped roasted peanuts and chopped fresh coriander, to garnish

sauce

1 tbsp preserved vegetables

½ tsp Szechuan peppers, lightly roasted and crushed

100 ml/3½ fl oz chicken stock

1 tsp black rice vinegar

1 tsp chilli oil

1 tsp dark soy sauce

1 tbsp light soy sauce

1 tbsp sesame paste

a few drops of sesame oil

2 spring onions, finely chopped

Dan Dan Noodles

Heat a wok over a medium–high heat, then add the groundnut oil. Toss in the chilli and Szechuan peppers, then add the meat and stir rapidly. When the meat has changed colour, add the light soy sauce and continue to cook until the meat is well browned.

Carefully mix together the sauce ingredients and pour into four individual serving dishes.

Soak the noodles in enough lukewarm water to cover for 15 minutes, or cook according to the packet instructions, until tender. Drain and divide among the serving dishes.

Top with the meat mixture, then sprinkle with the peanuts and coriander. Serve immediately.

SERVES 2–3

1½ tbsp Szechuan peppers
½ tsp salt
350 g/12 oz sirloin or rump steak
200 g/7 oz mixed small mushrooms, such as cremini, enoki and buna shimeji

½ tbsp cornflour
125 ml/4 fl oz Spicy Beef Stock (see page 9) or beef stock
2 tsp Chinese rice wine or dry sherry
4 tsp soy sauce
3 tbsp groundnut or vegetable oil

1 shallot, finely chopped
1 tsp finely chopped fresh ginger
1 large garlic clove, thinly sliced
3 tbsp chopped fresh coriander, to garnish

Beef with Mixed Mushrooms

Place the Szechuan peppers in a mortar with the salt and grind with a pestle. Sprinkle over both sides of the meat, pressing in well. Slice the meat diagonally across the grain into thin bite-sized pieces and set aside.

Wipe the mushrooms with damp kitchen paper. If using clumping mushrooms, such as enoki and buna shimeji, cut off the root and separate the clump. Cut any large mushrooms in half.

Mix the cornflour to a paste with 2 tablespoons of the stock. Add the rice wine and soy sauce, mixing well.

Heat a wok over a medium–high heat, then add 1 tablespoon of the oil. Fry the shallot and ginger for 1 minute. Add the garlic and fry for a few seconds, then add the mushrooms and 2 tablespoons of the stock. Stir-fry for 4 minutes. Add the cornflour mixture and the remaining stock. Bring to the boil, stirring, then reduce the heat and simmer for 2 minutes. Transfer to a warmed serving dish.

Wipe out the wok with kitchen paper, then heat over a high heat. Add the remaining oil. Add the beef and stir-fry for 3 minutes. Add to the mushroom mixture and sprinkle with the coriander. Serve immediately.

SERVES 4

2 tbsp groundnut or vegetable oil

225 g/8 oz shallots, roughly chopped

1 garlic clove, crushed

450 g/1 lb fillet steak, thickly sliced and cut into 2.5-cm/1-inch cubes

2 tbsp Masaman curry paste

3 potatoes, cut into 2.5-cm/1-inch cubes

400 ml/14 fl oz canned coconut milk

2 tbsp soy sauce

150 ml/5 fl oz beef stock

1 tsp palm sugar or soft light brown sugar

85 g/3 oz unsalted peanuts

handful of fresh coriander, chopped

cooked noodles, to serve

Masaman Curry

Heat a wok over a medium–high heat, then add the oil. Stir-fry the shallots and garlic for 1–2 minutes, until softened. Add the beef and curry paste and stir-fry over a high heat for 2–3 minutes, until browned all over.

Add the potatoes, coconut milk, soy sauce, stock and sugar and bring gently to the boil, stirring occasionally. Reduce the heat and simmer for 8–10 minutes, until the potatoes are tender.

Meanwhile, heat a separate dry frying pan until hot, add the peanuts and cook over a medium–high heat, shaking the frying pan frequently, for 2–3 minutes, until lightly browned. Add to the curry with the coriander and stir well. Serve immediately with noodles.

SERVES 4

500 g/1 lb 2 oz fillet steak, cut into thin strips
250 ml/9 fl oz groundnut or vegetable oil
3 celery sticks, cut into thin strips

1 red pepper, deseeded and cut into thin strips
1 fresh red chilli, deseeded and finely sliced
lime wedges, to serve

marinade
1 tsp salt
2 tbsp Thai fish sauce

Thai Marinated Beef with Celery

To make the marinade, mix the salt and fish sauce in a large bowl. Add the beef and toss to coat. Cover with clingfilm and put in the refrigerator for 1 hour to marinate.

Heat 225 ml/8 fl oz of the oil in a wok to 180–190°C/350–375°F, or until a cube of bread browns in 30 seconds. Deep-fry the beef in batches for 2–3 minutes, until crispy. Remove the wok from the heat and, using a slotted spoon, lift out the meat and drain it on kitchen paper.

Heat the remaining oil in the wok and stir-fry the celery, red pepper and chilli for 1 minute. Add the beef and cook for 2–3 minutes.

Serve immediately with lime wedges.

SERVES 4

groundnut or vegetable oil, for deep-frying
225 g/8 oz pork fillet, cut into 1-cm/½-inch cubes
1 onion, sliced
1 green pepper, deseeded and sliced
225 g/8 oz pineapple pieces
1 small carrot, cut into thin strips
25 g/1 oz canned bamboo shoots, drained and halved
cooked rice, to serve

batter
125 g/4½ oz plain flour
1 tbsp cornflour
1½ tsp baking powder
1 tbsp groundnut or vegetable oil

sauce
125 g/4½ oz soft light brown sugar
2 tbsp cornflour
125 ml/4 fl oz rice vinegar
2 garlic cloves, crushed
4 tbsp tomato purée
6 tbsp pineapple juice

Sweet & Sour Pork

To make the batter, sift the plain flour into a mixing bowl with the cornflour and baking powder. Add the oil and stir in enough water to make a thick, smooth batter (about 175 ml/6 fl oz).

Heat enough oil for deep-frying in a wok to 180–190°C/350–375°F, or until a cube of bread browns in 30 seconds. Dip the cubes of pork into the batter and deep-fry in batches until the pork is cooked through. Remove the pork from the wok with a slotted spoon and drain on kitchen paper. Set aside and keep warm until required.

Drain all but 1 tablespoon of oil from the wok and return it to the heat. Add the onion, green pepper, pineapple, carrot and bamboo shoots and stir-fry for 1–2 minutes. Remove from the wok with a slotted spoon and set aside.

Mix together all the sauce ingredients and pour into the wok. Bring to the boil, stirring until thickened and clear. Cook for 1 minute, then return the pork and vegetables to the wok. Cook for a further 1–2 minutes, then transfer to individual dishes and serve immediately with rice.

SERVES 4

500 g/1 lb 2 oz pork fillet, cubed
2 tbsp cornflour
3 tbsp soy sauce
1 tbsp rice vinegar
250 ml/9 fl oz water
2 tbsp groundnut or vegetable oil
2 leeks, thinly sliced

1 red pepper, deseeded and cut into thin strips
1 courgette, cut into thin strips
1 carrot, cut into thin strips
pinch of salt
cooked wild rice, to serve

marinade
1 tbsp soy sauce
pinch of chilli flakes

Szechuan-style Pork Stir-fry

To make the marinade, mix the soy sauce and chilli flakes in a bowl. Add the pork and toss to coat. Cover with clingfilm and leave to stand for 30 minutes.

Combine the cornflour, soy sauce and vinegar in a small bowl. Stir in the water gradually, then set aside. Heat a wok over a medium–high heat, then add the oil. Add the pork and marinade mixture and stir-fry for 2–3 minutes. Remove the pork from the wok with a slotted spoon and set aside.

Heat the remaining oil in the wok, add the leeks and red pepper and stir-fry for 2 minutes. Add the courgette, carrot and salt and stir-fry for a further 2 minutes.

Stir in the pork and the cornflour mixture and bring to the boil, stirring constantly, until the sauce thickens. Remove from the heat.

Serve immediately with wild rice.

SERVES 4

350 g/12 oz pork fillet, cubed
2 tbsp groundnut or vegetable oil
280 g/10 oz mushrooms, thinly sliced
1 courgette, thinly sliced
2 carrots, thinly sliced

115 g/4 oz canned bamboo shoots, drained
115 g/4 oz canned water chestnuts, drained and thinly sliced
1 garlic clove, crushed
125 ml/4 fl oz chicken stock
cooked rice, to serve

marinade
1 lemon grass stalk, finely sliced
2 tbsp Thai fish sauce
4 tbsp shredded fresh basil
juice of 1 lime

Pork with Basil & Lemon Grass

To make the marinade, mix the lemon grass, fish sauce, basil and lime juice in a bowl. Stir in the pork and toss well to coat. Cover with clingfilm and chill in the refrigerator for 1–2 hours.

Heat a wok over a medium heat, then add 1 tablespoon of the oil. Add the meat and the marinade and stir-fry until the pork is browned. Remove from the wok, set aside and keep warm.

Add the remaining oil to the wok and heat. Add all the vegetables and the garlic and stir-fry for about 3 minutes.

Return the pork to the wok and add the stock. Cook for 5 minutes, or until the stock is reduced.

Transfer to individual serving dishes and serve immediately with rice.

SERVES 4

225 g/8 oz dried wide rice noodles
2 tbsp groundnut or vegetable oil
4 spring onions, roughly chopped
2 garlic cloves, crushed
2 fresh red chillies, deseeded and sliced

225 g/8 oz pork fillet, trimmed and thinly sliced
115 g/4 oz large cooked peeled prawns
juice of 1 lime
2 tbsp Thai fish sauce
2 eggs, beaten

55 g/2 oz fresh beansprouts
handful of fresh coriander, chopped
55 g/2 oz unsalted peanuts, chopped
lime wedges, to serve

Pad Thai

Soak the noodles in a large saucepan of boiling water, covered, for 10 minutes, or according to the packet instructions, until tender. Drain, rinse under cold running water and set aside.

Heat a wok over a medium–high heat, then add the oil. Add the spring onions, garlic and chillies and stir-fry for 1–2 minutes. Add the pork and stir-fry over a high heat for 1–2 minutes, until browned all over.

Add the prawns, lime juice, fish sauce and eggs and stir-fry over a medium heat for 2–3 minutes, until the eggs have set and the prawns are heated through.

Add the beansprouts, most of the coriander, the peanuts and the noodles and stir-fry for 30 seconds, until heated through. Transfer to individual serving plates, sprinkle over the remaining coriander and serve immediately with lime wedges.

SERVES 4

450 g/1 lb fresh lamb mince
2 garlic cloves, crushed
1 tsp cumin seeds
1 tsp ground coriander

1 red onion, sliced
finely grated rind and juice of 1 orange
2 tbsp soy sauce

1 orange, peeled and segmented
salt and pepper
snipped fresh garlic chives, to garnish

Stir-fried Lamb with Orange

Heat a wok with a lid, without adding any oil. Add the lamb to the wok. Dry fry the lamb for 5 minutes, or until the lamb is evenly browned. Drain away any excess fat from the wok.

Add the garlic, cumin seeds, coriander and onion to the wok and stir-fry for a further 5 minutes.

Stir in the orange rind and juice and the soy sauce, mixing until thoroughly combined. Cover, reduce the heat and leave to simmer, stirring occasionally, for 15 minutes.

Remove the lid, increase the heat and add the orange segments. Stir to mix. Season to taste with salt and pepper and heat through for a further 2–3 minutes.

Transfer the stir-fry to individual serving plates and garnish with garlic chives. Serve immediately.

SERVES 4

450 g/1 lb lean boneless lamb (leg or loin fillet)
2 tbsp groundnut or vegetable oil
2 fresh bird's eye chillies, deseeded and finely chopped
2 garlic cloves, crushed

4 shallots, chopped
2 lemon grass stalks, sliced
6 fresh kaffir lime leaves
1 tbsp tamarind paste
2 tbsp palm sugar or soft light brown sugar

300 ml/10 fl oz canned coconut milk
175 g/6 oz cherry tomatoes, halved
1 tbsp chopped fresh coriander, plus extra to garnish
cooked rice, to serve

Lamb with Lime Leaves

Using a sharp knife, cut the lamb into thin strips or cubes. Heat a wok over a high heat, then add the oil. Add the chillies, garlic, shallots, lemon grass, lime leaves, tamarind paste and sugar.

Add the lamb to the wok and stir-fry for 5 minutes, tossing well so that the lamb is evenly coated in the spice mixture.

Pour the coconut milk into the wok and bring to the boil. Reduce the heat and simmer for 20 minutes.

Add the cherry tomatoes and coriander to the wok and simmer for 5 minutes. Transfer to individual serving plates, sprinkle with coriander and serve immediately with rice.

SERVES 4

4 tbsp groundnut or vegetable oil
550 g/1 lb 4 oz lamb neck fillet, thinly sliced
1 large onion, finely chopped
2 garlic cloves, finely chopped

2 fresh red chillies, deseeded and thinly sliced
175 g/6 oz mangetout
350 g/12 oz spinach leaves, coarse stalks removed
2 tbsp lime juice

3 tbsp oyster sauce
2 tbsp Thai fish sauce
2 tsp caster sugar
5 tbsp chopped fresh mint
salt and pepper

Stir-fried Lamb with Mangetout & Spinach

Heat a wok over a high heat, then add the oil. Add the lamb and stir-fry for 2–3 minutes, or until browned all over. Remove with a slotted spoon and drain on kitchen paper.

Add the onion, garlic and chillies to the wok and stir-fry for 3 minutes. Add the mangetout and stir-fry for 2 minutes, then stir in the spinach and return the lamb to the wok.

Add the lime juice, oyster sauce, fish sauce and sugar and cook, stirring constantly, for 4 minutes, or until the lamb is cooked through and tender. Stir in the mint, season to taste with salt and pepper and serve immediately.

SERVES 4–6

4 tsp soy sauce
1 tbsp cornflour
1 tbsp Chinese rice wine or dry sherry
¼ tsp salt
350 g/12 oz skinless, boneless chicken breasts, cut into cubes
6 tbsp Basic Chinese Stock (see page 9) or chicken stock

1 tbsp oyster sauce
4 tbsp groundnut or vegetable oil
1 tsp finely chopped fresh ginger
1 large garlic clove, thinly sliced
4 spring onions, white and green parts separated, diagonally sliced into 2-cm/¾-inch pieces

½ tbsp white peppercorns, crushed
8 baby corn, diagonally halved
½ small red pepper, deseeded and thinly sliced
140 g/5 oz canned water chestnuts, drained
115 g/4 oz mangetout, diagonally halved

Peppered Chicken Stir-fry

In a small bowl, combine half the soy sauce, the cornflour, rice wine and salt. Put the chicken pieces in a shallow dish and pour over the soy sauce mixture, stirring to coat. Leave to stand for 15 minutes.

Mix the remaining soy sauce with the stock and oyster sauce, and set aside.

Heat a wok over a high heat, then add the oil. Add the chicken and stir-fry for 3 minutes, until no longer pink. Remove from the wok with a slotted spoon and drain on kitchen paper.

Reduce the heat slightly, then add the ginger, garlic, white spring onion and the crushed peppercorns and stir for a few seconds. Add the baby corn, red pepper and water chestnuts. Stir-fry for 2 minutes, then return the chicken to the wok. Add the mangetout and the soy sauce mixture and stir-fry for 1–2 minutes, until the sauce is thickened.

Sprinkle with the green spring onion and cook for a few more seconds. Serve immediately.

SERVES 4

2 tbsp groundnut or vegetable oil
1 garlic clove, chopped
3 spring onions, sliced
4 skinless, boneless chicken breasts, cut into bite-sized chunks

1 tbsp grated fresh ginger
½ tsp chilli powder
150 g/5½ oz mangetout
125 g/4½ oz baby corn

2 tbsp smooth peanut butter
1 tbsp light soy sauce
cooked rice, to serve

Chicken & Peanut Stir-fry

Heat a wok over a medium–high heat, then add the oil. Add the garlic and spring onions and stir-fry for 1 minute. Add the chicken, ginger and chilli powder and stir-fry for a further 4 minutes. Add the mangetout and baby corn and cook for 2 minutes.

In a bowl, mix together the peanut butter and soy sauce, then add it to the wok. Stir-fry for a further minute.

Remove from the heat, transfer to individual serving dishes and serve with rice.

SERVES 4

2 tbsp groundnut or vegetable oil
4 spring onions, roughly chopped
2 tbsp Thai green curry paste

700 ml/1¼ pints canned coconut milk
1 chicken stock cube
6 skinless, boneless chicken breasts, about 115 g/4 oz each, cut into 2.5-cm/1-inch cubes

large handful of fresh coriander, chopped
1 tsp salt
cooked rice, to serve

Thai Green Chicken Curry

Heat a wok over a medium–high heat, then add the oil. Add the spring onions and stir-fry for 30 seconds, or until starting to soften.

Add the curry paste, coconut milk and stock cube and bring gently to the boil, stirring occasionally. Add the chicken, half the coriander and the salt and stir well. Reduce the heat and simmer gently for 8–10 minutes, until the chicken is cooked through and tender. Stir in the remaining coriander. Serve immediately with rice.

SERVES 4

50 ml/2 fl oz chicken stock
2 tbsp soy sauce
2 tbsp Chinese rice wine or dry sherry
3 tsp cornflour
1 egg white, beaten
½ tsp salt

4 tbsp groundnut or vegetable oil
450 g/1 lb skinless, boneless chicken breast, cut into strips
450 g/1 lb mushrooms, thinly sliced
1 head of broccoli, cut into florets

150 g/5½ oz fresh beansprouts
100 g/3½ oz canned water chestnuts, drained and thinly sliced
175 g/6 oz pistachio nuts
cooked rice, to serve

Chicken with Pistachio Nuts

Combine the stock, soy sauce and rice wine with 1 teaspoon of the cornflour. Stir well and set aside.

Combine the egg white, salt, 2 tablespoons of the oil and the remaining cornflour. Toss and coat the chicken in the mixture.

Heat a wok over a high heat, then add the remaining oil. Add the chicken in batches and stir-fry until golden. Remove from the wok, drain on kitchen paper and set aside to keep warm.

Add the mushrooms and broccoli to the wok and cook for 2–3 minutes.

Return the chicken to the wok and add the beansprouts, water chestnuts and pistachio nuts. Stir-fry until all the ingredients are warmed through. Add the stock mixture and cook, stirring continuously, until thickened.

Serve immediately with rice.

SERVES 4

1 tbsp groundnut or vegetable oil
1 garlic clove, finely chopped
2.5-cm/1-inch piece fresh ginger, finely chopped
1 small fresh red chilli, deseeded and finely chopped

350 g/12 oz skinless, boneless chicken breasts, cut into thin strips
1 tbsp Thai seven-spice seasoning
1 red pepper and 1 yellow pepper, deseeded and sliced
2 courgettes, thinly sliced

225 g/8 oz canned bamboo shoots, drained
2 tbsp Chinese rice wine or dry sherry
1 tbsp light soy sauce
2 tbsp chopped fresh coriander, plus extra leaves to garnish
salt and pepper

Thai-spiced Chicken with Courgettes

Heat a wok over a high heat, then add the oil. Add the garlic, ginger and chilli and stir-fry for 30 seconds to release the flavours.

Add the chicken and Thai seasoning and stir-fry for about 4 minutes, or until the chicken has coloured all over. Add the peppers and courgettes and stir-fry for 1–2 minutes, or until slightly softened.

Stir in the bamboo shoots and stir-fry for a further 2–3 minutes, or until the chicken is cooked through and tender. Add the rice wine, soy sauce and salt and pepper to taste and sizzle for 1–2 minutes.

Stir in the chopped coriander and serve immediately, garnished with coriander leaves.

SERVES 4

2 boneless chicken breasts, with or without skin, cut into 1-cm/½-inch cubes
1 tbsp groundnut or vegetable oil
10 dried red chillies, or to taste, snipped into 2–3 pieces
1 tsp Szechuan peppers
3 garlic cloves, finely sliced
2.5-cm/1-inch piece fresh ginger, finely sliced
1 tbsp roughly chopped spring onion, white part only
85 g/3 oz roasted peanuts
cooked rice, to serve

marinade
2 tsp light soy sauce
1 tsp Chinese rice wine
½ tsp sugar

sauce
1 tsp light soy sauce
1 tsp dark soy sauce
1 tsp black rice vinegar
a few drops of sesame oil
2 tbsp chicken stock
1 tsp sugar

Gong Bau Chicken

Combine all the marinade ingredients in a bowl. Add the chicken, toss well and leave to marinate, covered, for at least 20 minutes. Combine all the ingredients for the sauce and set aside.

Heat a wok over a high heat, then add the groundnut oil. Stir-fry the chillies and Szechuan peppers until crisp and fragrant. Toss in the chicken pieces. When they begin to change colour, add the garlic, ginger and spring onion. Stir-fry for about 5 minutes, or until the chicken is cooked.

Pour in the sauce, mix together thoroughly, then stir in the peanuts. Serve immediately with rice.

SERVES 4

small knob of butter
2 large eggs, beaten
½ tbsp groundnut or
    vegetable oil
6 shallots, cut into
    quarters

450 g/1 lb cooked
    chicken, cubed
3 tbsp soy sauce
2 carrots, diced
1 celery stick, diced
1 red pepper, deseeded
    and diced

175 g/6 oz fresh peas
100 g/3½ oz canned
    sweetcorn, drained
275 g/9¾ oz cooked
    long-grain rice

Chicken Fried Rice

Heat the butter in a small heavy-based frying pan and add the beaten egg. Swirl the egg until it covers the base of the pan. Cook until the egg has set and is cooked through, then turn out onto a plate. Cut the omelette into strips.

Heat a wok over a medium heat, then add the oil. Add the shallots and fry until soft, then add the chicken and 2 tablespoons of the soy sauce and stir-fry for 5–6 minutes.

Stir in the carrots, celery, red pepper, peas and sweetcorn and stir-fry for a further 5 minutes. Add the rice and stir thoroughly.

Finally, stir in the omelette strips and the remaining tablespoon of soy sauce. Serve immediately.

SERVES 4

1 tbsp groundnut or vegetable oil
2 red onions, sliced
2 tbsp Penang curry paste
400 ml/14 fl oz canned coconut milk
150 ml/5 fl oz chicken stock
4 kaffir lime leaves, roughly torn

1 lemon grass stalk, finely chopped
6 skinless, boneless chicken thighs, chopped
1 tbsp Thai fish sauce
2 tbsp Thai soy sauce
1 tsp palm sugar or soft light brown sugar

50 g/1¾ oz unsalted roasted peanuts, chopped, plus extra to garnish
175 g/6 oz fresh pineapple, roughly chopped
15-cm/6-inch piece cucumber, peeled, halved lengthways, deseeded and thickly sliced

Penang Chicken Curry

Heat a wok over a medium–high heat, then add the oil. Add the onions and stir-fry for 1 minute. Add the curry paste and stir-fry for 1–2 minutes.

Pour in the coconut milk and stock. Add the lime leaves and lemon grass and simmer for 1 minute. Add the chicken and gradually bring to the boil. Simmer for 8–10 minutes, until the chicken is tender.

Stir in the fish sauce, soy sauce and sugar and simmer for 1–2 minutes. Stir in the peanuts, pineapple and cucumber and cook for 30 seconds. Serve immediately, sprinkled with extra peanuts.

SERVES 4

225 g/8 oz dried medium egg noodles
3 tbsp groundnut or vegetable oil
1 large garlic clove, thinly sliced
2 tsp finely chopped fresh ginger
450 g/1 lb turkey steaks, cut into thin strips

175 g/6 oz chestnut mushrooms, thinly sliced
600 g/1 lb 5 oz pak choi, stalks cut into 2.5-cm/1-inch squares and leaves sliced into wide ribbons

4 spring onions, green part included, diagonally sliced into 2.5-cm/1-inch pieces
1 tbsp light soy sauce
2 tbsp chopped fresh coriander
salt and pepper

Turkey with Pak Choi & Mushrooms

Cook the noodles in a saucepan of boiling water for 4 minutes, or according to the packet instructions, until tender. Drain, rinse and drain again, then leave to cool.

Heat a wok over a medium–high heat, then add the oil. Stir-fry the garlic and ginger for a few seconds to flavour the oil.

Add the turkey and stir-fry for 2 minutes, until no longer pink. Add the mushrooms and pak choi stalks and stir-fry for 2 minutes. Add the pak choi leaves and spring onions and stir-fry for a further 2 minutes. Stir in the noodles and soy sauce, and season to taste with salt and pepper. Cook until the noodles are heated through, then add the coriander. Serve immediately.

SERVES 4

15 g/½ oz stem ginger
2 tbsp groundnut or
  vegetable oil
450g/1 lb skinless,
  boneless turkey breast,
  cut into thin strips

50 g/1¾ oz fresh or frozen
  cranberries
100 g/3½ oz canned
  chestnuts

4 tbsp cranberry sauce
3 tbsp light soy sauce
salt and pepper

Stir-fried Turkey with Cranberry Glaze

Drain off the syrup from the stem ginger. Using a sharp knife, finely chop the ginger. Set aside.

Heat a wok over a medium–high heat, then add the oil. Add the turkey to the wok and stir-fry for 5 minutes, or until cooked through.

Add the ginger and cranberries to the wok and stir-fry for 2–3 minutes, or until the cranberries have softened.

Add the chestnuts, cranberry sauce and soy sauce, season to taste with salt and pepper and allow to bubble for 2–3 minutes.

Transfer to a serving dish and serve immediately.

SERVES 2

250 ml/9 fl oz water or chicken stock, plus extra if needed
100 g/3½ oz basmati rice
2 tsp groundnut or vegetable oil
1 small egg, beaten
100 g/3½ oz turkey steak, cut into thin strips

1 carrot, cut into thin lengths
4 spring onions, chopped
2 garlic cloves, crushed
1 fresh red chilli, deseeded and chopped

100 g/3½ oz cooked peeled prawns
50 g/1¾ oz fresh beansprouts
2 tsp soy sauce
pinch of caster sugar

Nasi Goreng

Bring the water to the boil in a saucepan and tip in the rice. Return to the boil, then reduce the heat to a simmer. Cover the pan and cook for 10–15 minutes, until the rice is tender and all the water has been absorbed.

Meanwhile, heat 1 teaspoon of the oil in a small heavy-based frying pan and add the beaten egg. Swirl the egg until it covers the base of the pan. Cook until the egg has set and is cooked through, then turn out onto a plate. Cut the omelette into strips.

When the rice is nearly cooked, heat a wok over a high heat, then add the remaining oil. Add the turkey and stir-fry for 1 minute. Add the carrot, spring onions, garlic and chilli, and stir-fry for a further 2 minutes.

Reduce the heat, add the cooked rice to the wok with the prawns, beansprouts, soy sauce and sugar and stir gently for 1–2 minutes. If the mixture sticks, add a little water or stock. Arrange the omelette strips on top and serve immediately.

SERVES 4

1 tsp Chinese five-spice seasoning
1 tbsp cornflour
4 skinless, boneless duck breasts, cut into thin strips
1 tbsp chilli oil

225 g/8 oz baby onions, peeled
2 garlic cloves, crushed
100 g/3½ oz baby corn
175 g/6 oz canned pineapple chunks, drained

6 spring onions, sliced
100 g/3½ oz fresh beansprouts
2 tbsp plum sauce

Fruity Duck Stir-fry

Mix the five-spice seasoning and the cornflour. Toss the duck in the mixture until well coated.

Heat a wok over a high heat, then add the oil. Stir-fry the duck for 10 minutes, or until just beginning to crispen around the edges. Remove from the wok and set aside.

Add the onions and garlic to the wok and stir-fry for 5 minutes, or until softened. Add the baby corn and stir-fry for a further 5 minutes. Add the pineapple, spring onions and beansprouts and stir-fry for 3–4 minutes. Stir in the plum sauce.

Return the cooked duck to the wok and toss until well mixed. Transfer to individual serving dishes and serve immediately.

SERVES 4

2 tbsp clear honey
4 tbsp soy sauce
4 skinless, boneless duck
breasts, sliced

1 tbsp groundnut or
vegetable oil
bunch of spring onions,
sliced

1 small head of Chinese
leaves, finely shredded
salt and pepper

Honeyed Duck Stir-fry

Combine the honey and soy sauce in a large bowl. Add the duck slices and toss to coat in the marinade.

Heat a wok over a high heat, then add the oil. Add the duck strips, reserving the marinade, and stir-fry for 2 minutes, until browned.

Add the spring onions, Chinese leaves and the reserved marinade. Cook for 3–4 minutes, until the duck is cooked but still a little pink in the centre.

Season to taste with salt and pepper and serve immediately.

Fish & Seafood

SERVES 4–6

½ tsp salt

450 g/1 lb thick white fish fillets, cut into 2.5-cm/1-inch cubes

2 dried Chinese mushrooms

3 tbsp groundnut or vegetable oil

2.5-cm/1-inch piece fresh ginger, finely shredded

1 tbsp chopped spring onion

1 red pepper, deseeded and cut into 2.5-cm/1-inch squares

1 green pepper, deseeded and cut into 2.5-cm/1-inch squares

25 g/1 oz canned bamboo shoots, drained and cut into small cubes

2 tsp Chinese rice wine

2 tbsp pine kernels, toasted

Fried Fish with Pine Kernels

Sprinkle the salt over the fish and set aside for 20 minutes. Soak the mushrooms in a bowl of warm water for 20 minutes. Squeeze out any excess water from the mushrooms and finely slice, discarding any tough stalks.

Heat a wok over a medium–high heat, then add 2 tablespoons of the oil. Fry the fish for 3 minutes. Drain and set aside.

Wipe out the wok with kitchen paper, then add the remaining oil. Toss in the ginger. Stir until fragrant, then add the spring onion, peppers, bamboo shoots, mushrooms and rice wine and cook for 1–2 minutes.

Finally, add the fish and stir to warm through. Sprinkle with the pine kernels and serve immediately.

SERVES 6

140 g/5 oz plain flour
6 flounder or tilapia fillets,
    about 175 g/6 oz each
4–6 tbsp groundnut or
    vegetable oil
2 large garlic cloves,
    thinly sliced

4 ripe tomatoes,
    quartered
1 tbsp Thai fish sauce
12 fresh dill sprigs,
    trimmed
12 fresh coriander sprigs,
    trimmed

12 fresh Thai basil leaves
salt and pepper
cooked rice and Sweet,
    Sour & Spicy Fish Sauce
    (see page 6), to serve

Crispy Fish with Stir-fried Tomatoes & Herbs

Put the flour in a sealable polythene bag with salt and pepper to taste. Add the fish and seal the bag, then shake to coat each fillet evenly.

Heat 2 tablespoons of oil in a frying pan over a high heat. Working in batches and adding extra oil as needed, fry the fillets for 5–7 minutes, or until golden and crisp on both sides. Transfer to a serving platter.

Heat a wok over a high heat, then add 1 tablespoon of oil. Add the garlic and stir-fry for 3–5 minutes, or until just golden. Add the tomatoes and fish sauce and stir-fry for 10 minutes, or until softened. Adjust the seasoning, adding salt and pepper if needed. Spoon the tomato mixture on top of the fish.

Wipe out the wok with kitchen paper, then heat 1 tablespoon of oil over a high heat. Add the dill, coriander and basil and stir-fry for 1–2 minutes, or until just wilted. Scatter the herbs over the tomatoes and fish. Serve with rice and Sweet, Sour & Spicy Fish Sauce.

SERVES 4

2 tbsp groundnut or vegetable oil
1 garlic clove, chopped
2 tbsp Thai green curry paste
1 small aubergine, diced

125 ml/4 fl oz canned coconut milk
2 tbsp Thai fish sauce
1 tsp palm sugar or soft light brown sugar
225 g/8 oz firm white fish fillets, cut into pieces

125 ml/4 fl oz fish stock
2 kaffir lime leaves, finely shredded
about 15 fresh Thai basil leaves
fresh dill sprigs, to garnish

Thai Green Fish Curry

Heat a wok over a medium heat, then add the oil. Add the garlic and cook until golden. Add the curry paste and stir-fry for a few seconds before adding the aubergine. Stir-fry for about 4–5 minutes, until soft.

Add the coconut milk, bring to the boil and stir until it thickens and curdles slightly. Add the fish sauce and sugar to the wok and stir well.

Add the fish and stock. Simmer for 3–4 minutes, stirring occasionally, until the fish is just tender. Stir in the lime leaves and basil, then cook for a further minute. Transfer to a serving dish and garnish with dill sprigs. Serve immediately.

SERVES 6

450 g/1 lb fresh bun or 225 g/8 oz dried fine rice noodles
70 g/2½ oz rice flour or plain flour
½ tsp ground turmeric

900 g/2 lb white fish fillets, such as tilapia or flounder, cut into 2-cm/¾-inch cubes
2 tbsp groundnut or vegetable oil, plus extra for deep-frying
4 spring onions, cut into 2.5-cm/1-inch lengths

50 g/1¾ oz dry-roasted unsalted peanuts
24 fresh Thai basil leaves
24 fresh dill sprigs, trimmed
24 fresh coriander sprigs, trimmed
salt and pepper

Rice Noodles with Fried Yellow Fish, Peanuts + Herbs

If the bun has been refrigerated, reheat in boiling water for 2 seconds. Drain the bun and divide among six individual serving bowls. If using rice noodles, cook according to the packet instructions, until tender. Transfer to individual serving dishes.

Put the flour and turmeric in a sealable polythene bag and season to taste with salt and pepper. Shake to mix well. Add the fish cubes, then seal the bag and shake to coat each fish cube evenly.

Heat enough oil for deep-frying in a wok to 180–190°C/350–375°F, or until a cube of bread browns in 30 seconds. Working in small batches, take a handful of fish cubes and shake off the excess flour, then lower into the hot oil. Deep-fry for 2–3 minutes, or until golden and crisp. Drain on kitchen paper. Divide the fried fish cubes equally among the serving dishes.

Heat a wok over a high heat, then add the 2 tablespoons of oil. Add the spring onions and peanuts and stir-fry for 1 minute. Add the basil, dill and coriander and stir-fry for 1–2 minutes, or until just wilted. Divide among the serving dishes and serve immediately.

SERVES 4

2 tbsp groundnut or vegetable oil, plus extra for brushing

juice and finely grated rind of 1 large lemon

4 cod or haddock steaks, about 140 g/5 oz each, skinned

paprika, to taste

salt and pepper

spiced noodles

250 g/9 oz dried medium egg noodles

2 garlic cloves, chopped

2.5-cm/1-inch piece fresh ginger, finely chopped

2 tbsp very finely chopped fresh coriander root

1 tbsp kecap manis (sweet soy sauce)

1 fresh red bird's eye chilli, deseeded and finely chopped

1 tbsp Thai fish sauce

Cod with Spiced Noodles

Preheat the grill to high. Put the noodles in a saucepan of boiling water and cook for 3 minutes, or cook according to the packet instructions, until tender. Drain, rinse with cold water and drain again, then set aside.

Mix 1 tablespoon of the oil with the lemon juice and brush over one side of each fish steak. Sprinkle with the lemon rind and paprika and season to taste with salt and pepper. Lightly brush a grill rack with oil, then place the fish on the rack and cook under the preheated grill for 8–10 minutes, until the flesh flakes easily.

Meanwhile, heat a wok over a high heat, then add the remaining oil. Add the garlic and ginger and stir-fry for about 30 seconds. Add the coriander root and kecap manis and stir around. Add the noodles and stir thoroughly so they are coated in the kecap manis. Stir in the chilli and fish sauce. Divide the spiced noodles among individual serving plates, top each with a fish steak and serve immediately.

SERVES 4

2 tsp groundnut or vegetable oil

450 g/1 lb monkfish fillets, cut into 2.5-cm/1-inch chunks

1 onion, thinly sliced

3 garlic cloves, finely chopped

1 tsp grated fresh ginger

225 g/8 oz fine tip asparagus

175 g/6 oz mushrooms, thinly sliced

2 tbsp soy sauce

1 tbsp lemon juice

Monkfish Stir-fry

Heat a wok over a medium–high heat, then add the oil. Add the fish, onion, garlic, ginger, asparagus and mushrooms. Stir-fry for 2–3 minutes.

Stir in the soy sauce and lemon juice and cook for a further minute. Remove from the heat and transfer to individual serving dishes. Serve immediately.

SERVES 4

4 monkfish fillets, about 115 g/4 oz each
25 g/1 oz rice flour or cornflour
6 tbsp groundnut or vegetable oil

4 garlic cloves, crushed
2 large fresh red chillies, deseeded and sliced
2 tsp palm sugar or soft light brown sugar

juice of 2 limes
grated rind of 1 lime
2–3 tbsp water
cooked rice and lime wedges, to serve

Monkfish with Lime & Chilli Sauce

Toss the fish in the flour, shaking off any excess. Heat a wok over a medium–high heat, then add the oil. Fry the fish on all sides until browned and cooked through, taking care when turning not to break it up.

Lift the fish out of the wok and keep warm. Add the garlic and chillies and stir-fry for 1–2 minutes, until they have softened.

Add the sugar, the lime juice and rind and water and bring to the boil. Simmer gently for 1–2 minutes, then spoon the mixture over the fish. Serve immediately with rice and lime wedges.

SERVES 2

4 mackerel fillets, with skin, about 450 g/1 lb in total
1 tsp finely chopped fresh ginger
½ tsp salt
4 tbsp groundnut or vegetable oil

2½ tbsp plain flour
2.5-cm/1-inch piece fresh ginger, finely shredded lengthways
3 spring onions, sliced
finely shredded Chinese leaves, to serve

sauce
2 tbsp light soy sauce
½ tsp sugar
2 tsp Chinese rice wine or dry sherry

Sautéed Mackerel with Ginger & Spring Onions

Slice the mackerel fillets in half crossways. Diagonally slash the skin of each piece once or twice. Combine the chopped ginger with the salt. Rub the mixture over both sides of the fish, rubbing it into the slashes and any crevices in the flesh. Leave to stand for 15 minutes.

Combine the sauce ingredients in a small bowl and set aside.

Heat a wok over a medium–high heat, then add the oil. Toss the mackerel fillets in the flour and add to the wok. Fry for 4 minutes, turning once. Pour the sauce over the fish, sprinkle with the shredded ginger and spring onions and fry for a further 2 minutes.

Place a mound of Chinese leaves on two individual serving plates, then top with the mackerel and sauce. Serve immediately.

SERVES 4

4 tuna steaks, about 115 g/4 oz each, cut into strips
225 g/8 oz dried medium egg noodles
1 tbsp toasted sesame seeds
2 spring onions, diagonally sliced

marinade
125 ml/4 fl oz teriyaki sauce
2 tsp clear honey
salt and pepper

stir-fry
1 tbsp vegetable oil
2 tsp sesame oil
1 carrot, cut into thin strips

2 heads of pak choi, stalks and leaves separated and finely sliced
1 yellow pepper, deseeded and cut into thin strips
2 garlic cloves, chopped
1 tbsp soy sauce

Teriyaki Tuna with Stir-fried Vegetables & Noodles

For the marinade, mix together the teriyaki sauce, honey, and salt and pepper to taste in a shallow dish. Add the tuna and turn to coat in the marinade. Cover with clingfilm and leave to marinate in the refrigerator for 1 hour, turning the tuna occasionally.

Cook the noodles according to the packet instructions, until tender. Drain well and set aside.

Meanwhile, preheat the grill to high. Line the grill pan with aluminium foil. Remove the tuna from the marinade, reserving the marinade, and arrange in the grill pan. Spoon over half the marinade and cook under the preheated grill for 1 minute. Turn over, spoon over the remaining marinade and cook for a further minute.

Heat a wok over a high heat, then add the oils. Stir-fry the carrot, pak choi stalks and yellow pepper for 2 minutes. Add the garlic and pak choi leaves and stir-fry for 1 minute. Add the soy sauce and a little water. Divide the noodles among four individual serving bowls. Top with the stir-fried vegetables, tuna and any cooking juices, and sprinkle with the sesame seeds and spring onions.

SERVES 4

450 g/1 lb salmon fillet, skinned
2 tbsp kecap manis (sweet soy sauce)
2 tbsp tomato ketchup

1 tsp rice vinegar
1 tbsp demerara sugar
1 garlic clove, crushed
4 tbsp groundnut or vegetable oil

450 g/1 lb leeks, thinly shredded
sliced fresh red chillies, to garnish

Stir-fried Salmon with Leeks

Using a sharp knife, cut the salmon into slices. Place the slices of salmon in a shallow non-metallic dish.

Mix together the kecap manis, tomato ketchup, vinegar, sugar and garlic in a small bowl. Pour the mixture over the salmon, toss well and leave to marinate for about 30 minutes.

Meanwhile, heat a wok over a medium–high heat, then add 3 tablespoons of the oil. Add the leeks to the wok and stir-fry for about 10 minutes, or until the leeks become crispy and tender.

Using a slotted spoon, carefully remove the leeks from the wok and transfer to warmed serving plates.

Add the remaining oil to the wok. Add the salmon and the marinade to the wok and cook for 2 minutes. Remove the salmon from the wok, spoon over the leeks, garnish with chillies and serve immediately.

SERVES 4

100 g/3½ oz baby corn
2 tbsp groundnut or
vegetable oil
1 red onion, sliced
1 orange pepper,
deseeded and sliced
1 green pepper,
deseeded and sliced

450 g/1 lb salmon fillet,
skinned
1 tbsp paprika
225 g/8 oz canned
pineapple chunks in
natural juice, drained
100 g/3½ oz fresh
beansprouts

2 tbsp tomato ketchup
2 tbsp soy sauce
2 tbsp Chinese rice wine
or dry sherry
1 tsp cornflour

Stir-fried Salmon with pineapple

Cut each baby corn in half. Heat a wok over a medium–high heat, then add the oil. Add the onion, peppers and baby corn to the wok and stir-fry for 5 minutes.

Cut the salmon into thin strips and place in a large bowl. Sprinkle with the paprika and toss well to coat.

Add the salmon to the wok together with the pineapple and stir-fry for a further 2–3 minutes, or until the fish is tender. Add the beansprouts to the wok and toss well.

Mix together the tomato ketchup, soy sauce, rice wine and cornflour. Add to the wok and cook until the juices start to thicken. Transfer to serving plates and serve immediately.

SERVES 4

1 tbsp groundnut or vegetable oil
150 g/5½ oz mangetout
150 g/5½ oz baby corn
1 large orange or yellow pepper, deseeded and thinly sliced

8 spring onions, halved lengthways
2 garlic cloves, crushed
2-cm/¾-inch piece fresh ginger, finely chopped

2 tbsp teriyaki marinade
100 g/3½ oz cashew nuts
400 g/14 oz large cooked peeled prawns
1 tbsp sesame oil

Teriyaki Prawns with Cashew Nuts

Heat a wok over a high heat, then add the groundnut oil. Add all the vegetables and stir-fry for 4 minutes, or until almost tender but still with a little bite. Add the garlic and ginger and stir-fry for 1 minute.

Add the teriyaki marinade, cashew nuts and prawns and stir-fry for 2 minutes.

Transfer to individual serving bowls, drizzle over the sesame oil and serve immediately.

SERVES 2

1 tbsp groundnut or
vegetable oil
115 g/4 oz raw prawns,
peeled and deveined

4 eggs, lightly beaten
1 tsp salt
pinch of white pepper

2 tbsp finely snipped
garlic chives, plus extra
to garnish

Prawns Fu Yung

Heat a wok over a high heat, then add the oil. Stir-fry the prawns until they begin to turn pink.

Season the beaten eggs with the salt and pepper and pour over the prawns. Stir-fry for 1 minute, then add the garlic chives.

Cook for a further 4 minutes, stirring all the time, until the eggs are cooked through but still soft in texture. Serve immediately, garnished with extra garlic chives.

SERVES 2

350 g/12 oz raw tiger
  prawns
1½ tbsp finely chopped
  fresh ginger
2 shallots, finely chopped
½ fresh green chilli,
  deseeded and finely
  chopped

4 tbsp groundnut or
  vegetable oil
3 tbsp chopped fresh
  coriander
cooked rice, to serve

tamarind sauce
1 tbsp tamarind paste
1 tbsp sugar
2 tsp oyster sauce
2 tbsp water
1 tsp Thai fish sauce

Tiger Prawns in Tamarind Sauce

Remove the heads and shells from the prawns, leaving the tails intact, and devein. Combine the ginger, shallots and chilli in a small bowl. Combine the sauce ingredients in a separate bowl.

Heat a wok over a high heat, then add the oil. When the oil is almost smoking, add the prawns and stir-fry for 3–4 minutes, until just pink. Remove from the wok and drain in a colander.

Pour off all but 2 tablespoons of oil from the wok. Stir-fry the ginger mixture for 1 minute. Add the sauce and stir for a few seconds until hot. Add the prawns and stir-fry for 1 minute, until the sauce is slightly reduced.

Transfer to individual serving dishes and sprinkle with the coriander. Serve immediately with rice.

SERVES 4

350 g/12 oz raw prawns
2 tbsp groundnut or
   vegetable oil
1–2 garlic cloves, crushed
bunch of spring onions,
   chopped
snipped fresh garlic
   chives, to garnish
lime wedges, to serve

chilli dipping sauce
2 tbsp treacle or
   molasses
6 tbsp rice vinegar
2 tbsp Thai fish sauce or
   light soy sauce

2 tbsp water
1 garlic clove, crushed
2 tsp grated fresh ginger
2 tsp finely chopped fresh
   red chilli

Garlic-sizzled Prawns with Chilli Dipping Sauce

Remove the heads and shells from the prawns, leaving the tails intact, and devein.
To make the sauce, heat the treacle, vinegar, fish sauce and water in a small
saucepan until boiling. Add the garlic, ginger and chilli and pour into a small
serving bowl.

Heat a wok over a high heat, then add the oil. Add the garlic and spring onions
and stir-fry for 2 minutes, then add the prawns and cook for a further 2–3 minutes,
until they have turned pink.

Transfer to a serving plate, garnish with garlic chives and serve with the chilli
dipping sauce and lime wedges.

SERVES 4

2 tbsp groundnut or vegetable oil
1 small red pepper, deseeded and diced
200 g/7 oz pak choi, stalks thinly sliced and leaves chopped
2 large garlic cloves, chopped

1 tsp ground turmeric
2 tsp garam masala
125 ml/4 fl oz hot vegetable stock
2 heaped tbsp smooth peanut butter
350 ml/12 fl oz canned coconut milk

1 tbsp tamari
250 g/9 oz dried fine rice noodles
280 g/10 oz large cooked peeled prawns
2 spring onions, finely shredded
1 tbsp sesame seeds

Malaysian-style Coconut Noodles with Prawns

Heat a wok over a high heat, then add the oil. Add the red pepper, pak choi stalks and garlic and stir-fry for 3 minutes. Add the turmeric, garam masala and pak choi leaves and stir-fry for a further minute.

Combine the hot stock and peanut butter in a heatproof bowl until the peanut butter has dissolved, then add to the wok with the coconut milk and tamari. Cook over a medium heat for 5 minutes, or until reduced and thickened.

Meanwhile, soak the noodles in a saucepan of boiling water for 3–4 minutes, or according to the packet instructions, until tender. Drain the noodles and rinse under cold running water. Add the noodles and prawns to the wok and cook, stirring frequently, for a further 2–3 minutes, until heated through.

Serve immediately, sprinkled with the spring onions and sesame seeds.

SERVES 4

3 tbsp groundnut oil
2 tbsp sesame oil
16 large scallops, halved
225 g/8 oz small shiitake
  mushrooms, tough
  stalks removed

175 g/6 oz mangetout,
  diagonally halved
2 tsp finely chopped fresh
  ginger
2 garlic cloves, finely
  chopped

2 tsp light soy sauce
juice of 1 lime
3 tbsp torn fresh
  coriander leaves
salt and pepper

Scallop, Mangetout & Mushroom Stir-fry

Heat a wok over a high heat, then add the oils. Stir-fry the scallops for 1 minute. Add the mushrooms and mangetout, and stir-fry for a further minute.

Add the ginger, garlic, soy sauce and a splash of water to moisten. Stir-fry for a further 1–2 minutes, until the vegetables are just tender.

Add the lime juice and coriander leaves and season to taste with salt and pepper. Divide among individual serving plates and serve immediately.

SERVES 4

1 tsp groundnut or vegetable oil
5-cm/2-inch piece fresh ginger, grated
1 tbsp finely grated lime rind
1 orange pepper, deseeded and sliced

1 red onion, thinly sliced
300 g/10½ oz scallops
115 g/4 oz wild mushrooms, such as chanterelle or chestnut mushrooms

50 ml/2 fl oz lime juice
1 tsp clear honey (optional)
1 tbsp soy sauce
115 g/4 oz pak choi, shredded

Scallop Stir-fry

Heat a wok over a high heat, then add the oil. Add the ginger and cook, stirring, for 1 minute.

Add the lime rind, orange pepper and onion and stir-fry for 3–4 minutes, or until the onion has softened. Add the scallops and mushrooms to the wok and stir-fry for 2 minutes.

Pour in the lime juice, add the honey, if using, and the soy sauce. Stir together, then add the pak choi and continue to cook for 2–3 minutes, or until the scallops are tender. Serve immediately.

SERVES 2

900 g/2 lb small clams, scrubbed

1 tbsp groundnut or vegetable oil

1 tsp finely chopped fresh ginger

1 tsp finely chopped garlic

1 tbsp fermented black beans, rinsed and roughly chopped

2 tsp Chinese rice wine

1 tbsp finely chopped spring onion

1 tsp salt (optional)

Clams in Black Bean Sauce

Discard any clams with broken shells and any that refuse to close when tapped. Set aside the remaining clams.

Heat a wok with a lid over a high heat, then add the oil. Stir-fry the ginger and garlic until fragrant. Add the black beans and cook for 1 minute.

Add the clams and rice wine and stir-fry for 2 minutes to combine all the ingredients. Cover and cook for about 3 minutes, or until the clams have opened. Discard any clams that remain closed. Stir in the spring onion and the salt, if using. Serve immediately.

SERVES 4

750 g/1 lb 10 oz squid, cleaned and tentacles discarded
1 large red pepper, deseeded
115 g/4 oz sugar snap peas
1 head of pak choi

1½ tbsp groundnut or vegetable oil
1 small fresh red bird's eye chilli, chopped
1 garlic clove, finely chopped
1 tsp grated fresh ginger
2 spring onions, chopped

sauce
3 tbsp black bean sauce
1 tbsp Thai fish sauce
1 tbsp Chinese rice wine or dry sherry
1 tbsp dark soy sauce
1 tsp brown sugar
1 tsp cornflour
1 tbsp water

Stir-fried Squid with Hot Black Bean Sauce

Cut the squid body cavities into quarters lengthways. Use the tip of a small, sharp knife to score a diamond pattern into the flesh without cutting all the way through. Pat dry with kitchen paper.

Cut the pepper into long, thin slices. Cut the sugar snap peas in half diagonally. Coarsely shred the pak choi.

To make the sauce, combine the black bean sauce, fish sauce, rice wine, soy sauce and sugar in a bowl. Blend the cornflour with the water and stir into the other ingredients in the bowl. Set aside.

Heat a wok over a high heat, then add the oil. Add the chilli, garlic, ginger and spring onions and stir-fry for 1 minute. Add the pepper slices and stir-fry for 2 minutes.

Add the squid and stir-fry for a further minute. Stir in the sugar snap peas and pak choi and cook for a further minute, or until wilted.

Stir in the sauce and cook, stirring constantly, for 2 minutes, or until the sauce thickens and clears. Serve immediately.

SERVES 4

3 tbsp groundnut or
vegetable oil
2 large fresh crabs,
cleaned, broken
into pieces and legs
cracked with a cleaver

55 g/2 oz fresh ginger,
cut into julienne strips
100 g/3½ oz spring
onions, chopped into
5-cm/2-inch lengths

2 tbsp light soy sauce
1 tsp sugar
pinch of white pepper

Stir-fried Fresh Crab with Ginger

Heat a wok over a high heat, then add 2 tablespoons of the oil. Stir-fry the crab for 3–4 minutes. Remove from the wok and set aside.

Heat the remaining oil in the wok, add the ginger and stir until fragrant. Add the spring onions, then stir in the crab pieces. Add the soy sauce, sugar and pepper. Cover and simmer for 1 minute. Serve immediately.

SERVES 4

2 tbsp groundnut or vegetable oil
1 large onion, chopped
1 garlic clove, finely chopped
8 large tomatoes, peeled, deseeded and chopped

225 g/8 oz paella or risotto rice
about 850 ml/1½ pints fish stock
450 g/1 lb mussels, scrubbed and debearded

400 g/14 oz frozen mixed seafood, thawed
175 g/6 oz petit pois, cooked
2 tbsp chopped fresh parsley, plus extra to garnish
salt and pepper

Quick Seafood Rice

Heat a wok over a high heat, then add the oil. Add the onion and fry until just softened. Add the garlic and half the tomatoes and stir together well. Add the rice and stir-fry for 2–3 minutes, then add half the stock and bring to the boil. Simmer for 12–15 minutes, adding more stock as necessary.

Discard any mussels with broken shells and any that refuse to close when tapped. Add the remaining mussels to the wok with the mixed seafood and petit pois. Season to taste with salt and pepper and cook for a further 3–4 minutes, until hot, the mussels have opened and the liquid has been mostly absorbed. Discard any mussels that remain closed.

Stir in the remaining tomatoes and the parsley. Taste and adjust the seasoning, adding salt and pepper if needed. Serve immediately, garnished with extra parsley.

SERVES 4

115 g/4 oz white fish fillets, such as monkfish
2 tbsp groundnut or vegetable oil
1 fresh jalapeño chilli, deseeded and finely chopped
2.5-cm/1-inch piece fresh ginger, grated

85 g/3 oz raw prawns, peeled and deveined
115 g/4 oz baby corn, halved lengthways
115 g/4 oz mangetout
6 spring onions, chopped
1 tbsp soy sauce

115 g/4 oz squid, cleaned and cut into thin slices
115 g/4 oz spinach leaves, coarse stalks removed
115 g/4 oz fresh beansprouts

Seafood Stir-fry

Discard any skin from the fish, rinse lightly and pat dry on kitchen paper. Cut into small pieces.

Heat a wok over a high heat, then add the oil. Add the chilli and ginger and stir-fry for 1 minute, then add the fish and prawns and stir-fry for 2 minutes.

Add the baby corn, mangetout, spring onions and soy sauce and continue to stir-fry for 2–3 minutes, or until the fish is just cooked and the prawns have started to turn pink.

Add the squid, spinach and beansprouts and continue to stir-fry for a further 2 minutes, or until the fish, prawns and squid are cooked. Serve immediately.

SERVES 4

200 g/7 oz squid, cleaned and tentacles discarded

500 g/1 lb 2 oz firm white fish fillet, such as monkfish or halibut

12 clams, scrubbed

1 tbsp groundnut or vegetable oil

4 shallots, finely chopped

2 garlic cloves, finely chopped

2 tbsp Thai green curry paste

2 small lemon grass stalks, finely chopped

1 tsp shrimp paste

450 ml/16 fl oz canned coconut milk

200 g/7 oz raw king prawns, peeled and deveined

8 fresh basil leaves, finely shredded, plus extra leaves to garnish

Spicy Thai Seafood Stew

Using a sharp knife, cut the squid body cavities into thick rings and the white fish into bite-sized chunks. Discard any clams with broken shells and any that refuse to close when tapped.

Heat a wok over a medium–high heat, then add the oil. Add the shallots, garlic and curry paste and stir-fry for 1–2 minutes. Add the lemon grass and shrimp paste, then stir in the coconut milk and bring to the boil.

Reduce the heat until the liquid is simmering gently, then add the squid, white fish and prawns to the wok and simmer for 2 minutes.

Add the clams and simmer for a further minute, or until the clams have opened. Discard any clams that remain closed.

Sprinkle the shredded basil over the stew. Transfer to individual serving bowls, then garnish with basil leaves and serve immediately.

SERVES 4

115 g/4 oz dried wide rice noodles

2 tbsp groundnut or vegetable oil

6 spring onions, cut into 2.5-cm/1-inch lengths

1 large carrot, cut into matchsticks

55 g/2 oz French beans, cut into short lengths

2 tbsp Thai red curry paste

700 ml/1¼ pints canned coconut milk

225 g/8 oz skinned white fish fillets, such as cod or coley, cut into 2.5-cm/1-inch cubes

225 g/8 oz squid, cleaned and cut into thick rings

225 g/8 oz large raw prawns, peeled and deveined

55 g/2 oz fresh beansprouts

handful of fresh coriander, chopped

fresh Thai basil leaves, to garnish

Mixed Fish & Coconut Curry

Cook the noodles according to the packet instructions, until tender. Drain well and set aside.

Heat a wok over a medium–high heat, then add the oil. Add the spring onions, carrot and beans and stir-fry for 2–3 minutes, until starting to soften.

Stir in the curry paste, then add the coconut milk. Bring gently to the boil, stirring occasionally, then reduce the heat and simmer for 2–3 minutes. Add all the fish and seafood and the beansprouts and simmer for 2–3 minutes, until just cooked through and the prawns have turned pink.

Stir in the cooked noodles and coriander and cook for 1 minute. Serve immediately, garnished with basil leaves.

Vegetables

SERVES 2

1 butternut squash, weighing about 500 g/1 lb 2 oz
6 large shiitake mushrooms
5 tbsp groundnut or vegetable oil

½ tsp white peppercorns, crushed
½ tsp coriander seeds, crushed
2 large garlic cloves, thinly sliced
finely grated rind of ½ lemon

½ tbsp rice vinegar
4 tbsp chicken or vegetable stock
2 handfuls of baby spinach leaves, coarse stalks removed
salt

Stir-fried Butternut Squash

Cut the squash in two between the neck and the rounded part. Remove the skin from each piece. Quarter the rounded part and remove the seeds and fibres. Slice lengthways into thin segments. Slice the neck in half lengthways, then crossways into thin semicircles.

Remove and discard the tough stalks from the mushrooms and thinly slice the caps.

Heat a wok over a medium–high heat, then add the oil. Add half the peppercorns and half the coriander seeds. Stir for a few seconds, then add the squash in small batches. Fry for 5–7 minutes, carefully turning with tongs, until lightly browned and just tender. Sprinkle with salt to taste. Using a slotted spoon, transfer to a large sieve set over a bowl.

Add the mushrooms to the wok and fry for 4–5 minutes. Add the garlic and lemon rind and fry for a further minute. Sprinkle with salt to taste and the remaining peppercorns and coriander seeds. Add to the squash.

Pour any oil drained from the vegetables into the wok. Stir in the vinegar and stock and simmer for a few seconds, until slightly reduced.

Arrange the spinach in individual serving bowls. Pile the vegetables on top, then pour over the juices from the wok. Serve immediately.

SERVES 4

1 tbsp groundnut or vegetable oil
4 spring onions, finely sliced
1 carrot, cut into thin strips
1 courgette, cut into thin strips

½ head of broccoli, cut into florets
450 g/1 lb oyster mushrooms, thinly sliced
2 tbsp crunchy peanut butter

1 tsp chilli powder, or to taste
3 tbsp water
cooked rice, to serve
lime wedges, to garnish

Oyster Mushroom Stir-fry with Peanut Chilli Sauce

Heat a wok over a medium–high heat, then add the oil. Stir-fry the spring onions for 1 minute. Add the carrot and courgette and stir-fry for 1 minute, then add the broccoli and cook for a further minute.

Stir in the mushrooms and cook until they are soft and at least half the liquid they produce has evaporated. Add the peanut butter and stir well. Season with the chilli powder to taste. Finally, add the water and cook for a further minute.

Serve immediately with rice, garnished with lime wedges.

SERVES 4

2 tbsp groundnut or vegetable oil
2 onions, thinly sliced
bunch of fine asparagus spears
400 ml/14 fl oz canned coconut milk

2 tbsp Thai red curry paste
3 fresh kaffir lime leaves
225 g/8 oz baby spinach leaves, coarse stalks removed
2 heads of pak choi, chopped

1 small head of Chinese leaves, shredded
handful of fresh coriander, chopped
cooked rice, to serve

Thai Red Curry with Mixed Leaves

Heat a wok over a medium–high heat, then add the oil. Add the onions and asparagus and stir-fry for 1–2 minutes.

Add the coconut milk, curry paste and lime leaves and bring gently to the boil, stirring occasionally. Add the spinach, pak choi and Chinese leaves and cook, stirring, for 2–3 minutes, until wilted. Add the coriander and stir well. Serve immediately with rice.

SERVES 4

4 tbsp groundnut or vegetable oil
2 garlic cloves, chopped
1 onion, sliced
115 g/4 oz baby corn, diagonally halved
½ cucumber, peeled, halved, deseeded and sliced

225 g/8 oz canned water chestnuts, drained
55 g/2 oz sugar snap peas
115 g/4 oz shiitake mushrooms, halved
1 red pepper, deseeded and thinly sliced

1 tbsp palm sugar or soft light brown sugar
2 tbsp Thai soy sauce
1 tbsp Thai fish sauce
1 tbsp rice vinegar
8–12 fresh Thai basil sprigs
cooked rice, to serve

Mixed Vegetables with Quick-fried Basil

Heat a wok over a medium–high heat, then add half the oil. Stir-fry the garlic and onion for 1–2 minutes. Add the baby corn, cucumber, water chestnuts, sugar snap peas, mushrooms and red pepper and stir-fry for 2–3 minutes, until starting to soften.

Add the sugar, soy sauce, fish sauce and vinegar and gradually bring to the boil. Simmer for 1–2 minutes.

Meanwhile, heat a separate wok over high heat, then add the remaining oil. Add the basil sprigs and cook for 20–30 seconds, until crisp. Remove with a slotted spoon and drain on kitchen paper.

Transfer the vegetable stir-fry to individual serving plates and garnish with the crispy basil. Serve immediately with rice.

SERVES 4

3 tbsp groundnut or
vegetable oil
8 spring onions, chopped
1 garlic clove, crushed
1 tbsp grated fresh ginger
1 head of broccoli, cut
into florets

1 orange or yellow
pepper, deseeded and
roughly chopped
125 g/4½ oz red
cabbage, shredded
125 g/4½ oz baby corn
175 g/6 oz portobello
mushrooms, thinly
sliced

200 g/7 oz fresh
beansprouts
250 g/9 oz canned water
chestnuts, drained
4 tsp light soy sauce,
or to taste

Classic Stir-fried Vegetables

Heat a wok over a high heat, then add the oil. Stir-fry three quarters of the chopped spring onions with the garlic and ginger for 30 seconds.

Add the broccoli, orange pepper and cabbage and stir-fry for 1–2 minutes. Mix in the baby corn and mushrooms and stir-fry for a further 1–2 minutes.

Finally, add the beansprouts and water chestnuts and cook for 2 minutes. Pour in the soy sauce and stir well.

Serve immediately, garnished with the remaining spring onions.

SERVES 4

750 g/1 lb 10 oz fresh kale
2 tbsp groundnut or vegetable oil
1 onion, chopped
4 large garlic cloves, finely chopped
2 red peppers, deseeded and thinly sliced

1 large carrot, coarsely grated
100 g/3½ oz tiny broccoli florets
pinch of chilli flakes (optional)
125 ml/4 fl oz vegetable stock

115 g/4 oz mixed sprouted beans
handful of toasted cashew nuts, chopped
salt and pepper
lemon wedges, to serve

Kale Stir-fry

Using a sharp knife, remove any thick central cores from the kale. Stack several leaves on top of each other, then cut across them to shred finely. Repeat until all the kale is shredded, then set aside.

Heat a wok with a lid over a high heat, then add the oil. Add the onion and stir-fry for about 3 minutes, then add the garlic, peppers and carrot and continue stir-frying until the onion is tender and the peppers are starting to soften.

Add the broccoli and chilli flakes, if using, and stir. Add the kale to the wok and stir. Add the stock and salt and pepper to taste, reduce the heat to medium, cover the wok and simmer for about 5 minutes, until the kale is tender.

Remove the lid and allow any excess liquid to evaporate. Use two forks to mix the sprouted beans through the other ingredients, then adjust the seasoning, adding salt and pepper if needed. Transfer to individual serving plates and sprinkle over the cashew nuts. Serve immediately with lemon wedges.

SERVES 2-3

2 tbsp sesame oil
3 tbsp groundnut oil
200 g/7 oz small shiitake mushrooms
2 heads of pak choi, leaves left whole, stalks sliced

150 g/5½ oz mangetout, diagonally halved
250 g/9 oz tofu, drained and cubed
3-cm/1¼-inch piece fresh ginger, thinly sliced

2 garlic cloves, finely chopped
1 tbsp soy sauce
1 tsp sesame seeds
salt and pepper
cooked noodles, to serve

Mangetout, Sesame & Tofu Stir-fry

Heat a wok with a lid over a medium–high heat, then add the oils. Add the mushrooms, pak choi stalks and mangetout, and stir-fry for 1 minute.

Add the tofu, pak choi leaves, ginger, garlic and a splash of water to moisten. Stir-fry for a further 1–2 minutes, until the pak choi leaves have wilted.

Stir in the soy sauce, sprinkle with the sesame seeds and season to taste with salt and pepper. Serve immediately with noodles.

SERVES 4

1 onion, roughly chopped
3 garlic cloves, thinly sliced
2.5-cm/1-inch piece fresh ginger, thinly sliced
2 fresh green chillies, deseeded and finely chopped

1 tbsp groundnut or vegetable oil
1 tsp ground turmeric
1 tsp ground coriander
1 tsp ground cumin
1 kg/2 lb 4 oz mixed vegetables, such as cauliflower, courgettes, potatoes, carrots and French beans, cut into chunks

200 g/7 oz coconut cream or canned coconut milk
salt and pepper
2 tbsp chopped fresh coriander, to garnish
cooked rice, to serve

Vegetable & Coconut Curry

Put the onion, garlic, ginger and chillies in a food processor and process until almost smooth.

Heat a wok with a lid over a medium heat, then add the oil. Add the onion mixture and cook, stirring constantly, for 5 minutes.

Add the turmeric, coriander and cumin and cook, stirring frequently, for 3–4 minutes. Add the vegetables and stir to coat in the spice paste.

Add the coconut cream to the vegetables, cover and simmer for 30–40 minutes, until the vegetables are tender.

Season to taste with salt and pepper, garnish with the coriander and serve with rice.

SERVES 4

2 tbsp groundnut or
  vegetable oil
2 shallots, chopped
2 garlic cloves, crushed
225 g/8 oz basmati rice
about 600 ml/1 pint
  chicken stock

1 tbsp Thai red curry
  paste
1 tsp Thai fish sauce
3 tbsp soy sauce
175 g/6 oz baby corn,
  halved lengthways
115 g/4 oz baby carrots,
  halved lengthways

55 g/2 oz sugar snap
  peas
55 g/2 oz fresh
  beansprouts
4 tbsp sesame seeds
handful of fresh
  coriander, chopped
2 tbsp sesame oil
salt

Spring Vegetable Rice

Heat a wok over a medium–high heat, then add the groundnut oil. Add the shallots and garlic and stir-fry for 1–2 minutes. Add the rice and stir-fry for 2–3 minutes.

Add the stock, curry paste, fish sauce and soy sauce and bring to the boil, stirring occasionally. Reduce the heat and simmer for 10–12 minutes, until the rice is tender, adding more stock or boiling water, if necessary.

Meanwhile, cook the baby corn and carrots in a saucepan of lightly salted boiling water for 2–3 minutes, until just tender. Add the sugar snap peas and cook for 1 minute. Add the beansprouts and stir well, then drain.

Heat a dry frying pan until hot, add the sesame seeds and cook over a medium-high heat, shaking the frying pan frequently, for 30–45 seconds, until lightly browned.

Add the drained vegetables, coriander and sesame oil to the rice and mix well. Serve immediately, scattered with the toasted sesame seeds.

SERVES 4

150 ml/5 fl oz vegetable stock
2.5-cm/1-inch piece fresh galangal, sliced
2 garlic cloves, chopped
1 lemon grass stalk (white part only), finely chopped

2 fresh red chillies, deseeded and chopped
4 carrots, cut into chunks
225 g/8 oz pumpkin, peeled, deseeded and cut into cubes
2 tbsp vegetable or groundnut oil

2 shallots, finely chopped
3 tbsp Thai yellow curry paste
400 ml/14 fl oz canned coconut milk
4–6 fresh Thai basil sprigs
25 g/1 oz toasted pumpkin seeds, to garnish

Carrot + Pumpkin Curry

Pour the stock into a large saucepan and bring to the boil. Add the galangal, half the garlic, the lemon grass and chillies and simmer for 5 minutes. Add the carrots and pumpkin and simmer for 5–6 minutes, until tender.

Meanwhile, heat a wok over a medium–high heat, then add the oil. Stir-fry the shallots and the remaining garlic for 2–3 minutes. Add the curry paste and stir-fry for 1–2 minutes.

Stir the shallot mixture into the saucepan and add the coconut milk and Thai basil. Simmer for 2–3 minutes. Transfer to individual serving bowls and serve immediately, sprinkled with the toasted pumpkin seeds.

SERVES 2

1½ tbsp light soy sauce
1 tbsp oyster sauce
2 tbsp chicken stock or
Basic Chinese Stock
(see page 9)
groundnut or vegetable
oil, for deep-frying
350 g/12 oz firm tofu,
cubed

2 large garlic cloves,
thinly sliced
115 g/4 oz mangetout,
diagonally halved
4 spring onions,
diagonally sliced into
2.5-cm/1-inch pieces
115 g/4 oz fresh
beansprouts

salt and pepper
½ bunch of garlic chives,
snipped into 2.5-cm/
1-inch lengths,
to garnish
a few drops of sesame oil,
to serve

Stir-fried Tofu with Beansprouts

Combine the soy sauce, oyster sauce and stock in a small bowl and set aside.

Heat enough groundnut oil for deep-frying in a wok to 180–190°C/350–375°F, or until a cube of bread browns in 30 seconds. Add the tofu and deep-fry for 5–7 minutes, until golden brown, turning with tongs. Remove with a slotted spoon and drain on kitchen paper. Season to taste with salt and pepper.

Pour the oil from the wok, reserving 1 tablespoon, and wipe out the wok with kitchen paper. Heat the reserved oil, add the garlic and stir-fry for a few seconds to flavour the oil. Add the mangetout and spring onions and stir-fry for 2 minutes.

Add the beansprouts and soy sauce mixture. Stir-fry for 1 minute, then toss in the fried tofu and stir to mix. Transfer to individual serving bowls and scatter over the garlic chives. Drizzle with the sesame oil and serve immediately.

SERVES 2

140 g/5 oz dried wide rice noodles
6 tbsp soy sauce
2 tbsp lemon juice
1 tsp granulated sugar

½ tsp cornflour
1 tbsp groundnut or vegetable oil
2 tsp grated fresh ginger
2 garlic cloves, chopped
4–5 spring onions, sliced

2 tbsp Chinese rice wine or dry sherry
200 g/7 oz canned water chestnuts, drained and sliced

noodle Stir-fry

Put the noodles in a large bowl, cover with boiling water and soak for 4 minutes, or cook according to the packet instructions, until tender. Drain and rinse under cold running water.

Combine the soy sauce, lemon juice, sugar and cornflour in a small bowl.

Heat a wok over a medium–high heat, then add the oil. Add the ginger and garlic and stir-fry for 1 minute. Add the spring onions and stir-fry for 3 minutes.

Add the rice wine, followed by the soy sauce mixture and cook for 1 minute.

Stir in the water chestnuts and noodles and cook for a further 1–2 minutes, or until heated through. Serve immediately.

SERVES 4

2 tbsp groundnut or
  vegetable oil
6 spring onions, sliced
3 garlic cloves, crushed
1 red pepper, deseeded
  and diced
1 green pepper,
  deseeded and diced

1 fresh red chilli,
  deseeded and sliced
2 tbsp chopped water
  chestnuts
1 courgette, chopped
125 g/4½ oz oyster
  mushrooms

3 tbsp black bean sauce
2 tsp Chinese rice wine or
  dry sherry
4 tbsp dark soy sauce
1 tsp dark brown sugar
2 tbsp water
1 tsp sesame oil

Eight-jewel Vegetables

Heat a wok over a high heat, then add the groundnut oil. Reduce the heat slightly, add the spring onions and garlic and stir-fry for about 30 seconds.

Add the peppers, chilli, water chestnuts and courgette to the wok and stir-fry for 2–3 minutes, or until the vegetables are just beginning to soften.

Add the mushrooms, black bean sauce, rice wine, soy sauce, sugar and water to the wok and stir-fry for a further 4 minutes.

Drizzle over the sesame oil and serve immediately.

SERVES 4

2 tbsp groundnut or vegetable oil
450 g/1 lb carrots, grated
225 g/8 oz leeks, shredded

2 oranges, peeled and segmented
2 tbsp tomato ketchup
1 tbsp demerara sugar

2 tbsp light soy sauce
100 g/3½ oz peanuts, chopped

Carrot & Orange Stir-fry

Heat a wok over a high heat, then add the oil. Add the carrots and leeks to the wok and stir-fry for 2–3 minutes, or until the vegetables are just soft.

Add the orange segments to the wok and heat through gently, ensuring that you do not break up the orange segments as you stir the mixture.

Combine the tomato ketchup, sugar and soy sauce in a small bowl. Add the tomato ketchup mixture to the wok and stir-fry for a further 2 minutes.

Transfer the stir-fry to individual serving bowls and scatter over the peanuts. Serve immediately.

SERVES 4

6 dried Chinese mushrooms

275 g/9¾ oz firm tofu, drained

3 tbsp vegetable oil, plus extra for deep-frying

1 carrot, cut into thin strips

125 g/4½ oz mangetout

125 g/4½ oz baby corn, halved lengthways

225 g/8 oz canned bamboo shoots, drained and sliced

1 red pepper, deseeded and cut into chunks

125 g/4½ oz Chinese leaves, shredded

1 tbsp soy sauce

1 tbsp black bean sauce

1 tsp sugar

1 tsp cornflour

250 g/9 oz dried fine rice noodles, broken into 7.5-cm/3-inch lengths

Crispy Noodle, Vegetable & Tofu Stir-fry

Soak the mushrooms in a bowl of warm water for 20 minutes. Drain, reserving the soaking liquid. Squeeze out the excess water from the mushrooms and slice thinly, discarding any tough stalks.

Cut the tofu into cubes, then boil in a pan of lightly salted water for 2–3 minutes to firm up. Drain well. Heat a wok with a lid over medium–high heat, then add 1½ tablespoons of the oil. Add the tofu and fry until lightly browned. Remove and drain on kitchen paper.

Add the remaining 1½ tablespoons of the oil to the wok and stir-fry the mushrooms, carrot, mangetout, baby corn, bamboo shoots and red pepper for 2–3 minutes. Add the Chinese leaves and tofu and continue to stir-fry for a further 2 minutes. Stir in the soy sauce, black bean sauce and sugar.

Combine 6 tablespoons of the reserved mushroom liquid with the cornflour, then add to the wok. Bring to the boil, reduce the heat, cover and simmer for 2–3 minutes, until the sauce thickens slightly.

Heat enough oil for deep-frying in a wok to 180–190°C/350–375°F, or until a cube of bread browns in 30 seconds. Deep-fry the noodles, in batches, for 1½–2 minutes, or until crisp and puffed up. Drain on kitchen paper and serve with the stir-fry.

SERVES 4

2 aubergines, peeled
6 tbsp groundnut or
  vegetable oil
2 red peppers, deseeded
  and cut into thin strips
100 g/3½ oz canned
  water chestnuts,
  drained and sliced
6 spring onions, sliced
2 tsp finely chopped fresh
  ginger

1 large garlic clove, thinly
  sliced
1 fresh green chilli,
  deseeded and finely
  chopped
150 ml/5 fl oz hot
  vegetable stock
sesame seeds and thinly
  sliced spring onions,
  to garnish

sauce
1½ tbsp soy sauce
1½ tbsp rice vinegar
2 tsp sugar
2 tsp cornflour, blended
  to a smooth paste with
  a little water

Aubergine Stir-fry with Hot & Sour Sauce

For the sauce, combine the soy sauce, vinegar and sugar in a small bowl, stirring to dissolve the sugar. Mix in the cornflour paste and stir until smooth.

Slice the aubergines in half lengthways. With the flat side facing down, slice each half lengthways into 1-cm/½-inch strips. Slice the wider strips lengthways in half again, then cut all the strips crossways into 4-cm/1½-inch pieces.

Heat a wok over a high heat, then add 5 tablespoons of the oil. Add the aubergine and red peppers and stir-fry for 2–3 minutes, until just beginning to colour. Remove from the wok and drain on kitchen paper.

Heat the remaining tablespoon of oil in the wok over a high heat. Stir-fry the water chestnuts, spring onions, ginger, garlic and chilli for 1 minute.

Return the aubergine and red pepper to the wok. Reduce the heat to medium and add the sauce and stock. Stir-fry for 2–3 minutes, until slightly thickened. Sprinkle with sesame seeds and spring onions. Serve immediately.

SERVES 2

2 tsp groundnut or
  vegetable oil
a few drops of sesame oil
1 small garlic clove, finely
  chopped
pinch of Chinese
  five-spice seasoning
1 carrot, diced

2 baby corn, halved and
  thinly sliced
2 tbsp water
small handful of baby
  spinach, coarse stalks
  removed, finely sliced
175 g/6 oz cooked brown
  or white rice, chilled

dash of soy sauce
1 tsp sesame seeds
  (optional)
small knob of butter
1 egg, beaten

Chinese Rice with Omelette Strips

Heat a wok over a medium–high heat, then add the oils. Add the garlic, five-spice seasoning, carrot and baby corn and stir-fry for 5 minutes, stirring and tossing constantly to prevent the spices and vegetables from burning and sticking.

Add the water and stir-fry for 2 minutes, then mix in the spinach and cook, stirring frequently, for a further 2 minutes, or until the vegetables are tender.

Add the rice and soy sauce to the wok and heat through. Mix in the sesame seeds, if using.

Meanwhile, melt the butter in a small heavy-based frying pan and add the egg. Swirl the egg until it covers the base of the pan. Cook until the egg has set and is cooked through, then turn out onto a plate. Cut the omelette into strips or pieces.

Transfer the rice to individual serving bowls and arrange the omelette on top.

SERVES 4-6

2 eggs
½ tsp salt
pinch of white pepper
small knob of butter
2 tbsp groundnut or
    vegetable oil

1 tsp finely chopped
    garlic
1 small onion, finely sliced
1 green pepper, finely
    sliced
450 g/1 lb cooked rice,
    chilled

1 tbsp light soy sauce
1 tbsp finely chopped
    spring onion
140 g/5 oz fresh
    beansprouts
dash of sesame oil

Egg Fu Yung

Beat the eggs with the salt and pepper. Heat the butter in a small heavy-based frying pan and add the beaten egg. Swirl the egg until it covers the base of the pan. Cook until the egg has set and is cooked through, then turn out onto a plate. Cut the omelette into strips or pieces.

Heat a wok over a medium–high heat, then add the groundnut oil. Stir-fry the garlic until fragrant. Add the onion and stir-fry for 1 minute, then add the green pepper and stir for a further minute. Stir in the rice and, when the grains are separated, stir in the soy sauce and cook for 1 minute.

Add the spring onion and omelette strips, stir well, and finally add the beansprouts and sesame oil and stir-fry for 1 minute. Serve immediately.

SERVES 4

2 tbsp groundnut or
  vegetable oil
6 spring onions, chopped
2 garlic cloves, chopped
2 fresh green chillies,
  deseeded and
  chopped

450 g/1 lb courgettes, cut
  into thick slices
115 g/4 oz shiitake
  mushrooms, halved
55 g/2 oz fresh
  beansprouts
85 g/3 oz cashew nuts,
  toasted

a few fresh garlic chives,
  snipped
4 tbsp Thai soy sauce
1 tsp Thai fish sauce
cooked rice noodles,
  to serve

Courgette & Cashew Nut Curry

Heat a wok over a medium–high heat, then add the oil. Stir-fry the spring onions, garlic and chillies for 1–2 minutes, until softened but not browned.

Add the courgettes and mushrooms and cook for 2–3 minutes, until tender.

Add the beansprouts, cashew nuts, garlic chives, soy sauce and fish sauce and stir-fry for 1–2 minutes.

Serve immediately with rice noodles.

SERVES 4

300 g/10½ oz dried fine soba (buckwheat) noodles
3 tbsp groundnut or vegetable oil
1 tsp ground ginger
1 tbsp rice vinegar
1½ tsp sesame oil

1 tsp light soy sauce
100 g/3½ oz fresh beansprouts
85 g/3 oz mangetout, thinly sliced
4 spring onions, chopped
2 garlic cloves, crushed
1 red pepper, deseeded and very thinly sliced

½ head of cabbage, thinly shredded
small handful of fresh coriander leaves
pepper
toasted sesame seeds, to garnish

Wok-fried Soba Noodles

Cook the noodles in a saucepan of boiling water for 3 minutes, or according to the packet instructions, until tender. Drain well, then add to a bowl of cold water and use your hand to swish around to remove all the starch. Drain again, then put into another bowl of cold water and set aside.

Put 2 tablespoons of the groundnut oil into a large bowl and stir in the ginger. Beat in the vinegar, sesame oil and soy sauce. Add pepper to taste.

Drain the noodles very well, shaking off any excess water, then add to the bowl with the oil mixture. Add the beansprouts, mangetout, spring onions, garlic, red pepper and cabbage and use your hands to mix together. Season to taste with pepper. If you're not cooking immediately, cover the bowl with clingfilm and chill in the refrigerator until 10 minutes before you want to cook.

Heat a wok over a medium–high heat, then add the remaining groundnut oil. Tip in the noodles and vegetables and stir-fry for 3–5 minutes, until all the vegetables are hot and just tender. Add the coriander leaves and stir them through.

Transfer the noodles and vegetables to individual serving bowls and sprinkle with the sesame seeds. Serve immediately.

SERVES 2

450 g/1 lb mixed small mushrooms, such as cremini, enoki and buna shimeji
6 tbsp groundnut or vegetable oil
1 tsp coriander seeds, crushed
1 fresh bay leaf
175 g/6 oz French beans
1 large garlic clove, thinly sliced
3 tbsp lemon juice
2 tsp soy sauce
2 tbsp chopped fresh coriander
2 tsp sesame oil
2 tsp sesame seeds
salt and pepper

Mushrooms + French Beans with Lemon + Coriander

Wipe the mushrooms with damp kitchen paper. If using clumping mushrooms, such as enoki and buna shimeji, cut off the root and separate the clump. Cut any large mushrooms in half.

Heat a wok over a medium–high heat, then add the groundnut oil. Add the coriander seeds and bay leaf, and fry for a few seconds to flavour the oil. Add the mushrooms and beans and stir-fry for 5 minutes.

Stir in the garlic, lemon juice and soy sauce. Season to taste with salt and pepper and stir-fry for 2 minutes. Sprinkle with the coriander, sesame oil and sesame seeds and fry for a few seconds. Serve immediately.

SERVES 4

115 g/4 oz French beans
115 g/4 oz mangetout
115 g/4 oz carrots
115 g/4 oz asparagus
   spears
½ red pepper, deseeded

½ orange pepper,
   deseeded
½ yellow pepper,
   deseeded
2 celery sticks
3 spring onions
2 tbsp groundnut or
   vegetable oil

1 tsp finely chopped fresh
   ginger
2 garlic cloves, finely
   chopped
115 g/4 oz broccoli florets
salt

Summer Stir-fry

Slice the French beans, mangetout, carrots, asparagus, peppers, celery and spring onions and reserve. Heat a wok over a medium–high heat, then add half the oil. Add the ginger and garlic and stir-fry for a few seconds, then add the French beans and stir-fry for 2 minutes.

Add the mangetout, stir-fry for 1 minute, then add the broccoli florets, carrots and asparagus and stir-fry for 2 minutes.

Add the remaining oil, the peppers, celery and spring onions and stir-fry for a further 2–3 minutes, or until all the vegetables are just tender. Season to taste with salt and serve immediately.

SERVES 4

900 g/2 lb waxy potatoes
2 tbsp groundnut or
 vegetable oil
1 yellow pepper,
 deseeded and diced
1 red pepper, deseeded
 and diced
1 carrot, cut into
 matchsticks

1 courgette, cut into
 matchsticks
2 garlic cloves, crushed
1 fresh red chilli, sliced
bunch of spring onions,
 halved lengthways
125 ml/4 fl oz canned
 coconut milk

1 tsp chopped lemon
 grass
2 tsp lime juice
finely grated rind of 1 lime
1 tbsp chopped fresh
 coriander, plus extra
 to garnish

Thai Potato Stir-fry

Using a sharp knife, cut the potatoes into small cubes. Bring a large saucepan of water to the boil and cook the diced potatoes for 5 minutes. Drain thoroughly.

Heat a wok over a high heat, then add the oil. Add the potatoes, peppers, carrot, courgette, garlic and chilli to the wok and stir-fry for 2–3 minutes.

Stir in the spring onions, coconut milk, lemon grass and lime juice and stir-fry the mixture for a further 5 minutes.

Add the lime rind and coriander and stir-fry for 1 minute. Serve immediately, garnished with extra coriander.

SERVES 4

3 tbsp groundnut or vegetable oil
25 g/1 oz blanched almonds
1 large carrot, cut into thin strips
1 large turnip, cut into thin strips
1 onion, finely sliced

3 celery sticks, finely sliced
125 g/4½ oz Brussels sprouts, trimmed and halved
125 g/4½ oz cauliflower florets
1 garlic clove, crushed

125 g/4½ oz white cabbage, shredded
2 tsp sesame seeds
1 tsp grated fresh ginger
½ tsp chilli powder
1 tbsp chopped fresh coriander
1 tbsp light soy sauce
salt and pepper

Winter Vegetable Stir-fry

Heat a wok over a medium–high heat, then add the oil. Stir-fry the almonds until lightly browned, then lift them out and drain on kitchen paper. Set aside.

Add all the vegetables, except the cabbage, and the garlic to the wok and stir-fry briskly for 3–4 minutes.

Add the cabbage, sesame seeds, ginger and chilli powder and cook, stirring, for 2 minutes.

Stir in the coriander, soy sauce and the reserved almonds and season to taste with salt and pepper. Serve immediately.

SERVES 4

3 tbsp groundnut or
    vegetable oil
½ tsp ground turmeric
225 g/8 oz potatoes, cut
    into 1-cm/½-inch cubes
3 shallots, finely chopped
1 bay leaf
½ tsp ground cumin

1 tsp finely grated fresh
    ginger
¼ tsp chilli powder
4 tomatoes, roughly
    chopped
300 g/10½ oz spinach
    leaves, coarse stalks
    removed, roughly
    chopped

125 g/4½ oz fresh or
    frozen peas
1 tbsp lemon juice
salt and pepper
fresh coriander leaves,
    to garnish
cooked rice, to serve

Spicy Potato & Spinach Stir-fry

Heat a wok with a lid over a medium–high heat, then add 2 tablespoons of the oil. Stir in the turmeric and a pinch of salt. Carefully add the potatoes, stirring continuously to coat in the turmeric. Stir-fry for 5 minutes, then remove from the wok and set aside.

Heat the remaining tablespoon of oil in the wok and stir-fry the shallots for 1–2 minutes. Mix in the bay leaf, cumin, ginger and chilli powder, then add the tomatoes and stir-fry for 2 minutes.

Add the spinach, mixing well to combine all the flavours. Cover and simmer for 2–3 minutes. Return the potatoes to the wok and add the peas and lemon juice. Cook for 5 minutes, or until the potatoes are tender.

Remove the wok from the heat and discard the bay leaf, then season to taste with salt and pepper. Garnish with coriander leaves and serve immediately with rice.

SERVES 4

350 g/12 oz long-grain rice
1 tsp ground turmeric
2 tbsp groundnut or vegetable oil
225 g/8 oz courgettes, sliced
1 red pepper, deseeded and sliced

1 green pepper, deseeded and sliced
1 fresh green chilli, deseeded and finely chopped
1 carrot, coarsely grated
150 g/5½ oz fresh beansprouts

6 spring onions, sliced
2 tbsp soy sauce
salt
fresh coriander leaves, to garnish
lime wedges, to serve

Chinese Vegetable Rice

Place the rice and turmeric in a saucepan of lightly salted water and bring to the boil. Reduce the heat and leave to simmer until the rice is just tender. Drain the rice thoroughly and press out any excess water with a sheet of kitchen paper. Set aside until required.

Heat a wok over medium–high heat, then add the oil. Add the courgettes to the wok and stir-fry for about 2 minutes. Add the peppers and chilli and stir-fry for 2–3 minutes.

Stir the cooked rice into the mixture in the wok, a little at a time, tossing well after each addition. Add the carrot, beansprouts and spring onions to the wok and stir-fry for a further 2 minutes.

Drizzle over the soy sauce and stir well. Transfer to individual serving bowls and scatter over the coriander leaves. Serve immediately with lime wedges.